F. Gonzalez-Crussi, born and raised in Mexico City, received his M.D. degree from the National University of Mexico and pursued postgraduate training in pathology in the United States and Canada. Since 1978 he has been professor of pathology at Northwestern University as well as head of the Division of Anatomical Pathology at Children's Memorial Hospital in Chicago. He is the author of *Notes of an Anatomist*, *Three Forms of Sudden Death*, and more than ninety articles and has been published in French, Italian, Spanish, Dutch and Japanese. He is married to Dr Wei Hsueh, a medical researcher.

GW00724477

Also by F. Gonzalez-Crussi in Picador

Notes of an Anatomist
Three Forms of Sudden Death

F. GONZALEZ-CRUSSI

ON THE NATURE OF THINGS *Erotic*

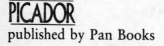
PICADOR
published by Pan Books

First published 1988 by Harcourt Brace Jovanovich
First published in Picador Hardback 1988 by Pan Books Ltd
This Picador edition published 1989 by Pan Books Ltd
Cavaye Place, London SW10 9PG

9 8 7 6 5 4 3 2 1

ISBN 0 330 31058 5

Printed and bound in Great Britain by
Cox & Wyman Ltd, Reading

To my wife, Wei, with gratitude

CONTENTS

ON THE NATURE OF
THINGS *Erotic*

EROS AMBIGUOUS, OR
THE OBSCURE OBJECT OF DESIRE

To begin at the beginning, it seems necessary to ask what is the nature of the sexual impulse, and why should it be that our kind is cleft in two sexes irresistibly drawn to each other. Various myths allow that the sexes were not always two, as they are now, but were originally three in number: man, woman, and a hybrid sex resulting from the combination of these two. Aristophanes says in the *Symposium* that the primeval race was made up of beings of peculiar somatic constitution called "Androgynous." An individual of the original race answered to this description: He was round, had two faces looking in opposite directions, and was equipped with two sets of limbs— four arms and four legs—by means of which he could displace himself frontward, backward, and sideways with the greatest of ease, speed, and agility. Wondrous to recount, the procreative parts of these individuals were also double. Of their love lives we have little information, but from this anatomic description it is valid to infer that they had a tendency to amorous intrigue of devilish complexity, and the need to enforce such rules as would secure the peaceful coexistence of the conjoined halves. The facts, however, showed their lack of restraint. The Androgynous race turned petulant and insolent. Great was their might, and they balked not at insulting the gods. It was this arrogance that brought about their downfall.

In less time than it takes to shout "hermaphrodite!," "gynandromorphic!," or some other expletive that the wrathful gods must have uttered, Zeus could have reduced the troublemakers to cinders with his thunderbolts. But this time Zeus was benevolent. Instead of obliterating the impudent, as would have been the just punishment for their disrespect, Zeus chose a subtler corrective measure. His decision was that all individuals belonging to the primitive human race would be cut in two from top to bottom along the median plane, as we slice a sorb apple with a knife, for pickling. After this measure was carried out, the victims were sobered and avowed themselves repentant. Men ought to have reckoned themselves fortunate for having learned their lesson opportunely. For, had they continued to direct their insolence toward the gods, Zeus was of a mind to split them anew. His contingency plan was to cut them again in two down the middle, so that men would have hopped around on one leg and would have looked like the figures of basso-relievo that we see sculpted on public monuments: two dimensional when viewed frontally and almost linear when seen in profile. It is enough that most men may be said "to lack depth" in a figurative sense; to be made to actually look the part would have been excessively harsh punishment.

Because the primeval human race learned its lesson after the first slicing, we look the way we look. After the divine surgery was completed, the gods did minor adjustments: The sectional plane was smoothed out and nicely worked to remove an unsightly hacked-off appearance; the skin was pulled over the cut surface and tied into a knot over the area that is now called the navel. Aristophanes adds that the generational organs were also transposed. What this means is simply beyond me, for I have never understood what was the arrangement of the genitals before the heavenly plastic surgery was practiced. The narrative is weak in terms of topographic anatomy. What is clear is that the original placement of the organs of generation determined certain practices among the primeval human beings that markedly differed from those now in vogue. Female eggs, for instance, were deposited in furrows on the ground, like those of insects, and the male sowed the seed upon the eggs thus externally deposited. But after the anatomical rearrangement took place, the genitalia came to be placed where they now exist, frontward and inferior to the belly.

A necessary functional consequence of the new anatomy was the need for mutual coordination and no small muscular dexterity when exercising the corresponding physiologic functions. Another consequence was that the mechanics of coupling (whatever braggart voluptuaries may tell us) were reduced to a very narrow range of expression. Indeed, Cyrene of Corinth was to achieve undying renown simply for having invented a dozen ways of making love: Aristophanes called her *dodekamikhanos,* or lady of the dozen variations. Heliogabalus reserved a generous portion of the national treasury, and valuable gifts, for any man or woman who would invent and demonstrate to the lubricious emperor any new way to stimulate his flagging lust, just as today we recompense citizens

3

who contribute to the good of society. A Greek woman author who lived in the first century B.C. and used the curious pen name of Elephantis toiled writing books on the subject, the most famous entitled *Katakliseis,* without succeeding in enlarging the measly repertoire. It is true that the oriental mind was particularly fertile in its concern for this domain of human life. The Indian sutras detailed the theoretical possibilities in poetical comparisons to tree and vine, river and rock, or other analogies from the world of nature. These researches were never widely divulged; at least among westerners, the Indian love manuals failed to raise a significant following. Not for lack of enthusiasm, to be sure, but because strict adherence to procedural rules endangered life and limb. For unless one is young, trained in yoga exercises, or versed in acrobatics, to sway under the gale of passion "like the rush bent by the storm" is hazardous to the musculoskeletal system.

The common man in ancient Greece seems not to have pondered unduly over the question of why individual human beings are powerfully driven to seek union with a mate. The explanation offered by the quaint myth was quite satisfactory: Human beings are actually halves of what they once were, and it is perfectly natural that one half should look for its complementary missing half. In one version, the original composite beings before their partition were formed of two portions of like sex; in another, of the aggregation of sexually discrepant parts. They could be doubly male, doubly female, or truly androgynous; which one was a matter of pure chance. The myth permits to account for the origin of homosexuality in the same stroke: Greek society needed to accommodate a frequently observed behavior into the logical, rationalistic climate that it extolled. Once the myth was believed, reason could be satisfied. Nothing surprising here: Reason must often rest upon blind belief, be it on an external, suprarational agency or on its own ability to lead us out of our perplexity.

Contemporary man turns to science for an explanation of our sexed nature. Scientific pronouncements are ambitious, for they address both the larger plan of evolution and the more restricted field of proximal causality. The former comes clothed in the noble terms of evolutionary biology, and may be developed as follows:

Consider a colony of protozoans leading their obscure lives in a pond. Their existence continues unperturbed as long as food remains plentiful. Those members of the protozoan community would be deemed successful who would most effectively gain access to the food. Basking in plenty, the business of living would go on unimpeded, and it is inevitable that the protozoans would soon divide. For, in the evolutionary perspective, success in biology is equivalent to "reproductive success." Assume, however, that nutriments become scarce. Reproduction would then take second place, like a luxury sacrificed by a well-to-do household that has fallen into bleak times. The formerly exulting protozoans would be forced into ways of life curiously analogous to those adopted by human beings during financial distress: emigration to a more promising environment or withdrawal into an austere, resource-conserving domicile, as in encystment. Sheer survival would have been attained, but in terms of biologic evolution these measures could be considered maladaptive: the routed protozoan had been shoved aside, reduced to a shadowy existence in which there is no offspring, a biologic limbo with no other prospects than to wait for the recurrence of circumstances that might permit a new attempt at perpetuating the species. And the future of the species would look equally grim, since the progeny would inherit the same limited resourcefulness with which to face environmental challenges.

One may speculate about another course of action open to the fortune-smitten protozoan. If it so much as aspires to the entrepreneurial spirit, it could undertake to restructure itself. For whenever simple, stereotyped somatic division is the sole manner of reproduction, the options bequeathed to the progeny—and thus the destiny of the race—are identical to those of the forebear. The possibility of renewal can come with reshuffling the individual's own genetic material or by uniting with another individual (whose genetic constitution is not identical to the sexual partner's). In either case greater genetic resourcefulness results. Instead of fixed, limited features to deal with the biologic struggle, new vistas are opened, and the potential for new ways to face the challenges is prodigiously enlarged. Hence the notion that sex was the outcome of the physiological advantage that results from combining two genetically diverse individuals; that it was one way of providing the variation indispensable for natural selection to act.[1]

Thus, to the instantaneous creation of a female companion out of the first man's rib or her cleaving off from a composite androgynous being, evolutionary theory opposes unfathomable millennia of dumb, striving, continuous organic development imprinting itself in the form of sexual differentiation. And all this for what purpose? Science tells us that at the bottom of all this there is a simple problem: the conservation of energy. In other words, sex is a problem of thermodynamics. In order to solve it, nature designed a motile cell and a stationary cell: The male sex cell ceaselessly wanders about, thereby increasing the chances of encountering a female recipient for transfer of genetic material (the sperm cell is, indeed, all genetic material and locomotion, and little else); the female cell, of equally admirable engineering design, is voluminous and passive, hardly able to move, as if made to save all the energy for fertilization while disdaining all other expenditure.

The cold formulations of science disappoint the romantic. Nowhere does one find in scientific literature the color and intensity that passionate spirits expect in a treatment of their favorite subject. Unless, of course, the scientist happens to be a romantic. In which case we are presented with a very different description of the protozoan reproductive cycle. Jean Rostand's work of scientific divulgation exemplifies such a romantic presentation. In *Le Bestiaire d'Amour,* he observes paramecia about to quit their manner of reproduction by binary fission and to engage in their brand of rudimentary sexuality: "They seem agitated, uneasy; swimming in all directions, as though in search of something, they collide, they strike one another with their cilia. . . ." The reader is led to understand, Love has abandoned his aerial habitat and, exchanging his proverbial arrows for some sort of diminutive, aquatic harpoons, decimates the swarms of unwary protozoans, who approach one another until the whole colony of paramecia trembles with courting and uniting couples. The investigator observes them through his microscope with the same aesthetic emotion with which an art critic contemplates the universal triumph of Love in Watteau's *Embarking for Cythera*. Paramecia, however, show less restraint than Watteau's polished couples, and with their impetuous effusions transform our observer from art dilettante to simple voyeur: These unicellular organisms embrace "mouth to mouth," and this caress is followed by still more intimate contact: "Their respective protoplasms blur, then fade at the forepart of the body, so that the two conjugant cells are now, so it seems, open to each other, in each other. This union takes about a quarter of an hour to achieve. The couple, which so far has been swimming, now sinks to the bottom of the water."

Note that the scientist's observations fail to give us the answer we covet. We wish to know what is the meaning of erotic attraction, but we are no closer to our goal. Haply we were made to believe that microscopic life is also swayed by the erotic, but we remain puzzled as to the nature of the force that draws paramecia together. It cannot be subsumed under the concept of "attraction of the sexes," since before the exchange of genetic material these organisms did not belong to opposite sexes, were not differentiated as male and female. Paramecial attraction is thus the attraction of bisexual beings, a particular instance of the myth of the Androgynous race. On the other hand, its purpose cannot be the reconstitution of a primitive Androgynous being, since bisexuality was already present in these protozoans—otherwise it would have been impossible for them to turn from simple division of their cell bodies to sexual reproduction, i.e., conjugation and interchange of nuclear substance. It is neither a drive toward the achievement of complementarity of opposites nor an impetus to reconstitute a primeval doubly sexed condition. Thus, the metaphysically inclined tend to conclude that the amorous impulse predates sexuality and is independent of it. The mutual attraction of living beings thus assumes the heroic, unmanageable dimensions of all things metaphysical: There is a universal force that impels living beings—and nonliving matter as well—to unite with each other. Sexuality inscribes itself, somewhat tardily and timidly, into this grandiose plan. It is neither logically necessary for procreation—nature amply demonstrates the superfluous quality of this mechanism—nor a fixed and immutable design. Sex is an accident. The romantic, once more, is shortchanged.

As to the "urgings of sex," that is, the proximate causes that impel multicellular sexed individuals to engage in procreation, science has never suffered for lack of explanations. The usual is to present us with a catalog of bodily juices, or endocrine secretions, that somehow explain, we are told, the physiological upheavals that relate to sexual life. The approach works well for the mechanics of coupling, but a universal theory of erotic love, I am afraid, cannot be wholly supported on neuroendocrinological explanations. Moreover, science makes no pretensions for total understanding. The nature of science is to raise new questions where old questions, now in ruins, once stood. Mating behavior in some species does not coincide with the greatest surge of sexual hormones: In the red-sided garter snake *(Thamnophis sirtalis parietalis)*, mating takes place when males have small testes and minimal circulating levels of sex hormones; copulatory behavior appears cued by changes in the ambient temperature, since males display courtship as they emerge from dormancy in the spring, whereas their gonads do not mature until the summer. For female Asian musk shrews *(Suncus murinus)*, sexual receptivity is greatest *before* the period of maximal ovarian function, whereas in males sexual behavior is clearly dependent upon hormonal levels. And for the desert-dwelling zebra finch *(Taeniopygia guttata castanotis)*, rain is the most potent aphrodisiac. The male zebra finch, though anatomically ready to engage in sexual activity, displays a complete indifference toward the female until rain falls. Then, naturalists plot the course of zebra finch behavior this way: Copulation occurs within ten minutes, nest-building within four hours, and egg-laying within a week after rain has fallen.[2]

It may not be useless to ask whether we carry in our ancestral memory the receptivity to changes in physical environment that these creatures manifest. Season of the year, time of the day, may not be wholly alien to human eroticism. Dante tells us in *Vita Nova* the precise timing, in astronomical terms, of his first encounter with Beatrice: "She had been in the world exactly the time that the starry sky employs to move one-twelfth of a degree toward the Orient." Had it not been shortly after the equinox of the spring of 1274, the experience may not have been so devastating. As it turned out, his young age (they were both nine years old, but in thirteenth-century Italy, we are compelled to admit, sexual maturation kept pace with the speed at which life was lived) was no impediment for the poet to feel that his whole body trembled at the sight of the girl; that blood ran faster in his veins; and that the secret chamber of his heart reverberated with the words "Here arriveth a god of greater strength than mine, who is come to subjugate me" *(Ecce deus fortior me, qui veniens dominabitur michi)*—that is, Love. By the same token, Beatrice appears to him to take him to Paradise under timing conditions that seem carefully, if somewhat cryptically, specified: "The lantern of the universe . . . [issued] from that [point] which joineth four circles in three crosses" *(Paradiso,* Canto I, 39). Some expositors have understood this to mean one week after the equinox, the circles being the line of the zodiac, the equator, and the equinoctial colure.[3] Thus, lovers live under the impression that cosmic influences converged to mark one day, or one hour, apart from all other divisions of time, as the time of their "fatal" encounter. If it were ever demonstrated that purely physical environmental changes account for their hormonal stirrings, I would not be the one to so inform them. And if lovers tell us that they feel that their lives are centered around one afternoon when they held hands under an umbrous bower; that at a certain hour the perfume of magnolias and daffodils diffused through the air, while a bird's song was heard; and that then—precisely at *that* instant—"their souls touched"; if they tell us all this, are we going to explain to them that their experience represents an instance of "environmental stimulation of gonadal recrudescence"? The true scientist, I fear, would not balk. Both the bird's song and the lovers' feeling that they live moments of exceptional significance may be accounted for under the same general theory. I read in my current issue of *Science* that "treatment of adult female canaries with androgens induces song behavior," and that sex steroid hormones actually change the structure of brain cells in experimental animals.[4]

Do we wish to consider the problem from the lofty heights of philosophy? We would be equally disappointed. Those who have most courageously grappled with the problem of Being seem to have taken little notice that "beings" often come in male and female versions. Traditional philosophy regarded our sexual nature as a purely contingent feature of our makeup. Indeed, sex appears at first sight as alien to the ontological problem discussed by metaphysicians: Being is something that antedates, so to speak, the anatomical and physiological differentiation of the body. "We are" is a proposition that can be made without regard for the sex of those who posit it; obviously, the proposition would be just as valid for men as for women. And yet, the view that relegates sexuality to the position of a secondary and accidental characteristic of human nature stands bluntly at odds with much of what has been learned of late. For today we know that human sexuality is much more than that set of physiological reactions by which the species is perpetuated. Sex is much more than the "combat of perspirations and pantings of the *opranti*" of which spoke

Valéry, and sex organs more than what he called *"la machine érotique"* (recently dismantled, exposed, and described with cool professional detail by Masters and Johnson). Modern psychology would present human sexuality as an integral part of the human condition, since it is present and manifest—in one form or another—from earliest infancy and does not disappear until the moment of death. Moreover, just as standing hair, sweating, accelerated cardiac beats, and pupillary changes do not account for the emotion of fear, so is the inventory of hormonal secretions, tumescence of genital organs, and other bodily changes notoriously incapable of delivering to us a rounded-up account of human sexual life. Hence, Sartre was justified in challenging the premise that sexuality is a contingent feature of human life, "an addition" to our being, and in advancing instead the radical statement that sex is at the center of the ontological problem. In his view, mankind is originally and fundamentally sexed. Man exists in the world as a sexed being not *because* he happens to have been granted a sex accidentally; rather, he is a sexed being because sex is a necessary structural arrangement for man to exist in the world as what he is, an entity capable of relating to other human beings.

But all this begs the question. If we are to reduce human eroticism to "a form of relating to others," the meaning of this relationship must be clarified. In the domain of differentiated sexuality, the concrete way of relating to others is that of "desire." This is a unique phenomenon that we have yet to even begin to understand. In vain did Stoics and Epicureans define sexual desire as an impulse toward pleasure, or the removal of a painful want. They failed to explain why it is that a man who desires sexually experiences desire toward *a woman*, rather than specifically desire of pleasure, or of ridding himself of a want. In truth, desire is a mysterious human riddle that has always wanted satisfactory definition. Sartre was the first to realize that by an error of perspective the average man deludes himself into thinking that sexual desire is the same as desire of coition. Elderly individuals, the impotent, or the young who lack knowledge of amorous practices nevertheless experience desire. As Sartre puts it, "Desire in no way implies by itself the sexual act, does not pose it thematically, does not even sketch it, as one sees in the case of young children, or adults ignorant of the 'technic' of love."[5]

There is more. It is obvious that to say that this desire is *desire of a body* is a partial, unsatisfactory answer. A body, of course, is the object of desire, but a body whose consciousness is active and oriented toward the solicitation of the subject who experiences desire. A body surrendered to us unconscious, under the effect of a drug, or coerced by fright or by violence is not, under normal circumstances, desirable. The Courts of Love of the twelfth century, supremely wise in the erotic, set it down as an article of their code of law that "there is no flavor in what a lover takes by force from the other lover" *(Non est sapidum quod amans ab invito sumit amante)*. A man may basely stoop to vent his sexual tensions under such conditions, but would not, ordinarily, describe this setting as desirable. A sadist, or a psychopath, may find that humiliation and fright in his partner is eminently a part of his erotic desire. Yet this deviant attitude would confirm that sexual desire is not merely "desire of a body," but of the organic totality of a body and its consciousness in a special relation to the world and to the subject who experiences desire.

And so we come to one of the oldest, but also least comforting, of the theories on the nature of the erotic. It views love as the imperialism of the soul, a tendency to impose our arbitrary rule on others. Lovers expect proofs, oaths, reiterated demonstrations. Desire, like love, is demanding: it expects the lover to surrender himself, and the lover's freedom to enslave itself by a kind of circular movement, like that of a snake biting its own tail. In a well-known episode of the court of King Francis I of France, the mistress of Lord De Lorge, captain of the Scots Guard, dropped one of her gloves into the pen where lions were kept in preparation for a lion fight that was to amuse the aristocrats in the courtyard. She asked De Lorge to go in and get it for her "if he loved her as much as he said." De Lorge rolled his cape around his forearm and entered the pen holding the tip of his sword against the lions. By sheer good luck, the beasts did not attack him. But when De Lorge went back to his mistress he broke the lovers' loop of enslavement: He flung the glove to her face, indignant at having been made to risk his life in what, in his newly acquired optics, seemed a futile and irrational act. In times of less civility than ours, women were often known for high-handedness in wielding this kind of erotic might. The mistress of Claude de Clermont-Tallard, nephew of Diane de Poitiers, demanded an equally barbarous token of her lover's devotion. Upon listening to his protestations, she said: "If you love me as much as you say, and are as brave as you claim, plunge your dagger in your arm for the love of me." The man drew his dagger and would have self-inflicted the atrocious wound but for the providential appearance of a friend, who grabbed his arm, took away the dagger, and persuaded him of the foolishness of that act.

Men, of course, were never paragons of generosity. To them, sexual desire and "possession" have long been associated concepts. In many languages, to gain sexual access to a female is synonymous with "possessing" her. Thus, for men, language reinforces the atavistic notion of eroticism as domination. This is why in male deviancy the symbolism of possession may be strikingly expressed. In 1985, the newspapers of the United States reported a sensational criminal case of sexual enslavement in which a man had kept a woman recluse inside a wooden contraption for several years. This extraordinary case is not unprecedented. The pathologic lover wishes to put his mistress in a state of utter material dependence: He is free to see her, to possess her at any hour of the day or night, according to his whim. The normal lover is no less strange, but in a different way: He seems to wish her free, and by a paradoxical movement wishes to "possess" her as a free agent. I am not referring here to a simple desire of dominance and subjugation. Note that the lover is not satisfied if his love object comes to him "willingly." "Willingly" is not enough, for the lover who knows that the woman has consented out of an ulterior motive, say, in payment of an important favor, or for money, is not fully gratified by her consent. Or the lover who obtains the woman's acquiescence without her enthusiasm: He is equally unfulfilled. The lover who knows that his pious mistress remains loyal to him only because her religious upbringing will not allow her to break the church vow that she once made feels frustrated and deceived: it is not enough for him that she stays "willingly." The Sartrian analysis is thus correct: The lover wishes "the freedom of the Other to determine itself to become love . . . and that this freedom become captive *of itself,* and that it turn back upon itself, as in madness, or in dreams, to wish its own captivity."

And having granted all this, it becomes necessary to ask why such an appetite would ever arise in us. What are we to do of this surrender of the Other? Can it be true that sexual desire is nothing more than the ingrained desire of appropriation of somebody's corporeal and psychic presence? But the sexual partner is another human being, that is to say, an active participant in whom the same or correlative desires are present. Is the theme of sexuality, then, that of a conflict, a pitting of two human beings warring to appropriate each other's intimate beings? If so, what is the purpose of this appropriation? But perhaps this interpretation is completely mistaken, and sexual love is not a form of conflict. This unromantic interpretation could not have gone unchallenged. Love as a struggle for dominance was anathema to a civilized age. A sentiment eager to exalt the other's welfare over one's own could not be likened to war and malicious strife. This is why the romantic faction worked out its own formulation: Not a struggle, but a synthesis, underlies the attraction of the sexes. The purpose of the erotic is not the subjugation of the weak by the autocratic and powerful, but the creation, out of the two commingled beings, of a new and more perfect entity. The myth of the Androgyne was revived.

It would be more accurate to say that the myth was reactivated. It was never dead. All human cultures have nurtured the idea of bisexual beings, in which distinction between male and female is effaced, leaving place to a bewildering duality. Traces of preoccupation with this myth are evident in the most disparate settings, from ancient Babylonian inscriptions to neoclassical French painting in the nineteenth century. Anywhere, and at any time, we are apt to discover its presence; for like all enduring myths, this one answers to mankind's deepest yearnings and anxieties. Its abiding nature, and its eternal fascination, stem from the elemental belief that our sexed nature arose out of a pristine, undivided whole to which we must return. The Androgyne represents this finished whole: a complete being that needs no other being to ensure its perpetuation. It is a total being, without deficiency or gap in the sexual sphere, and thus the very embodiment of immortality.

Not surprisingly, the Androgyne has been attractive and repulsive. The concrete expression of the myth has evoked awe, reverence, horror, or scandal. Among the ancient Greeks it took the form of an ideal vision, magnificently expressed in classical statuary. But when, in succeeding ages, the statues of the Greek Hermaphroditus were unearthed, the Christian diggers recoiled in revulsion. The splendid marbles of this male-female hybrid were to them an abomination, a satanic violation of that divine organizing principle by which all created things can be neatly ranged into a scheme of recognizable antithetical poles: hot and cold, black and white, moist and dry, weak and strong . . . male and female. Yet, the learned knew that religion itself had not escaped the influence of the myth. Side by side with Christian orthodoxy there flourished esoteric doctrines that maintained the existence of an androgynous deity responsible for the creation of an equally androgynous first man. Controversy raged for a long time over a cryptic biblical passage: "*Elohim* created man in his image. In the image of *Elohim* he created him. Male and female he created them." (Gen. 1:27.) Gnostics, neo-Platonists, cabalists, alchemists, and assorted propounders of esoteric doctrines took this to mean that a bisexed deity had fashioned man in his image and semblance. Grammatical imprecision, with its glaring discordance of gender and number in nouns and pronouns, was still an inviting target for Voltaire's pointed barbs. In his *Philosophical Dictionary* he pondered: "If god or the secondary gods created man male and female in their likeness, it would seem in that case that the Jews believed god and the gods to be males and females." Was it God alone, or God and celestial attendants, meant by the word *Elohim*? Fathers of the Catholic church suggested that reference to more than one divine person was implied and reiterated in the approving statement made after the creation of man was complete: "Adam is become as one of us." (Gen. 3:22.) Voltaire unforgivingly retorted: "There is no question of trinity in the Bible." Details of the controversy would be out of place here. Suffice it to say that esoteric doctrines admitted the synthesis of male and female essences in Adam, and therefore in God, in whose image man was created. To the joint male and female principles man owed, while in Eden, his domination of the world. The joint principles were dispersed and brought asunder as a result of the fall, but redemption will signify a reconstitution of the pristine condition, when in symbolic synthesis the Divine Unity will again be attained.

As the Adrogyne had been important for mystics and theologians, it became the subject of intense preoccupation for artists of more recent times. Already the refined aristocracy of the *ancien régime* could appreciate the formal splendor in the artistic Greco-Roman conception of androgynism. The Marquis de Sade encounters Hermaphroditus for the first time on a trip to Florence, in a famous gallery, and writes home immediately: "You know, Madame Countess, that the intemperance of ancient Romans dared to look for voluptuosity even in this kind of monster. This one is life-sized, recumbent on the abdomen, though a little to one side; he leans on his arms, in an attitude that allows to perceive a well-formed feminine bosom; the thighs are somewhat crossed, and hide altogether the other mark of the feminine sex; that of the male one is strongly expressed there; the body is beautiful, and the sublime proportions seem of the greatest truth." Hermaphroditus is still a "kind of monster," but already aesthetically "sublime."[6] An art historian of the era set the canon to judge of those artistic productions: Nature has imperfections, but the artist mends with industry the flaws of nature. "Art . . . tried to combine the beauties and properties of the two sexes in the figures of Hermaphroditus, which, such as we see them represented in the work of the ancient artists, are ideal productions."[7] This was the defined ideal for generations of artists: Like a diligent gardener who, not content with wild natural growths, grafts portions of some plants onto others, the artist transplants isolated parts of beautiful bodies to compose an ideal whole. Artistic conceptions changed, "currents" thrived and disappeared, but the theme of the Androgyne lived on. In the neoclassical "academic" painters who rendered the ambiguous body of Endymion, loose in slumber; in Canova's equally indeterminate, winged adolescent bodies; or in such novels as Balzac's *Séraphita* or Gautier's *Mademoiselle de Maupin,* the Androgyne continues to reveal itself as a living symbol, able at one time to inspire artistic productions and to confer upon them a rich philosophic and aesthetic meaning.

The relevance of the myth seems less obvious in our day. We are neither partial to theological subtleties nor fond of ambiguity in the plastic arts. Steeped in science and technology, contemporary man will not suffer talk on symbols. True, hermaphroditism is well known to science, but the gap is too wide between primitive life forms such as cestodes or trematodes, in which bisexuality is normal, and ourselves. Nor are we much disturbed by the knowledge that human sexual differentiation is a chancy matter; that human beings start off as androgynous beings during embryonic development; and that largely fortuitous mechanisms determine the orientation of monosexuality in one direction or another. Vestiges of our androgynous past are normally present in our bodies: Rudimental structures of the opposite sex are found in the mature individual. The discovery of sexual hormones did more to emphasize the similarity than the separation of the sexes. Male hormones are present in females, and female hormones in males; qualitatively identical hormones circulate in both sexes, differing only in their proportion. It is thus technically correct to say that some degree of androgynism is normal in human beings. Has this knowledge, backed by irreproachable scientific respectability, influenced the average man's ideas on the meaning of eroticism? Hardly. Attempt to elicit their opinions, if you would contemplate smugness and boredom in the flesh. Tell them that the perfect erotic relationship cannot be the coupling of the he-man and the she-woman, since both are figments of the collective imagination, lacking in scientific proof. Restrained yawning will salute this commonplace. Say that the purpose of the erotic is not complementarity of opposites, but the positive benefit that comes to a lover from finding, in the partner, the same strands as are present in his own personality. Yawns are now irrepressible. Fearing a thicker hail of platitudes, your interlocutors now take their leave. Each one goes back to the comfortable, familiar roles that society assigns to people of "well-defined sexuality," and not one more thought will be reserved for androgynism.

This complacency is ill advised. We should have known. We heard it from Aristophanes that the Androgynous race was not to be trusted. It could not be expected from the rascally lot that they would suffer our disdain without grumble. And they have not. Only this time they will not be content with the insubstantial status of a symbol, and they mean to exert unchecked empire on our lives. Take heed: The rule of androgynism is imminent. To accomplish this end, the Androgyne has enlisted in its service the radical fringes of feminism, as will be presently explained.

It is no secret that in the struggle for equality, women liberationists are divided. The apple of discord is maternity and what to do about it. It is an undeniable fact that women are the ones who have the babies; should they, on this reckoning, be treated differently from men? Should there be, say, special treatment for women under the law, as in the case of maternity leave from work? *Yea,* answer the conservatives, who rally behind such slogans as Betty Friedan's "Women Should Not Be Treated Like Male Clones."[8] *Nay,* votes the radical faction, distrustful of special treatments (and with good cause, since glorification of maternity has often conduced to subtle forms of feminine subjection). Equality is to be complete, insist the radicals. And one of their champions, Elisabeth Badinter, of France, foretells a future of *absolute* equality between the sexes, which amounts to no less than the dawn of the new Androgynous Reality. Interviewed by Italian reporters, she declared: "Only people of bad faith can maintain that men and women do not resemble each other more and more [as time passes]." The unisex fashion, inconceivable a generation ago, is now no cause for astonishment. But this is a trivial symptom. Consider the deeper manifestations: Men share more and more in the domestic tasks formerly assigned exclusively to women; many men are no longer ashamed to admit that they would be willing to stay at home, and take care of the house full time, if this were practical. The young are evolving new attitudes vis-à-vis man-woman relationships. No longer is it assumed for a moment that domination and possession have anything to do with erotic relationships. Not even complementarity of roles. The new theory of the erotic starts to develop the theme of perfect psychic (as well as physical) similarity: Love is a striving for complete identity—body and soul. To recapitulate the Sartrian analysis, we may ask: What will happen to desire, then? What are we to do with the thick farrago of notions that say that bodily attraction, or desire, is felt toward another body that is the "opposite," or at least the "complement," of our own? Here Badinter's reply is worth quoting in full: "It is men above forty who show the greatest hostility [to the central thesis of the androgynous future]. When they say 'passion,' or 'desire,' they mean conquest, possession. This worked admirably well until the end of the last century, when [erotic] love was still a conflictive relationship between two different individualities. Today the two sexes resemble each other greatly, and for the young the essential thing is not to seduce the partner in order to achieve his or her possession, but rather to find the perfect understanding, the maximal complicity, the utmost solidarity. How could it be otherwise in a world in which desire can be satisfied immediately? What means 'to possess' someone who gives himself or herself spontaneously?"[9]

Now, some men would admit to feeling jittery upon hearing this advocacy of absolute sexual equality. Most, however, would not stir from their usual dull apathy on this matter. And the reason is obvious: For as long as maternity is the woman's exclusive prerogative, all talk of real androgynism is idle. Maternity has been the impassable shoal in the course to feminist unity, and it is now the chief hindrance in thrusting androgynism from symbolic to real existence. But it will not be said that limitations of the flesh stood in the way of a feminist with a sense of destiny. Badinter, undaunted, announces the fall of the last barrier: The pregnant male, she proclaims in her latest manifesto, is a viable possibility. Not only imaginable, but also ripe, and even overdue, for actualization. That such an idea sparked an emotional conflagration is proof that the myth of the Androgyne is living and well, thank you, in contemporary society. Badinter's announcement triggered no small an emotional storm among her readers.[10] The idea of male pregnancy seemed to some amusing, to others preposterous, and to still others outright obscene. It is nonetheless worthy of our consideration.

No one who has been exposed to the practice of obstetrics would gainsay that maternity may be eminently suitable for some fathers. The interest that they take in the proceedings is unrivaled, and many, no doubt, are more intensely affected by pregnancy and delivery than the mothers. Scarcely can it be denied that among those men, especially the young ones, are many who would be wonderful childbearers. "Ah, yes, but . . ." starts the obligatory reply to these considerations, punctuated by a half-bemused, half-sarcastic smile. Remember, however, that a womb is not indispensable for the fetus to develop. Pregnancy has proceeded to term, albeit infrequently, outside the uterus; the placenta may implant on the peritoneum, and yet the fetus may attain the stage of viability. An exquisitely monitored interplay of hormones is required during gestation. But the endocrinology of pregnancy is very well known. If a team of scientists meant to reproduce this hormonal environment in a male, my guess would be that they would succeed. Recollect that the entire human genome is now being mapped. Consider that today conception may be avoided by taking a morning pill; ovulation induced by a similar method; sperm frozen for long periods without loss of inseminating potency; early embryonic development successfully maintained in a test tube; the sex of the progeny chosen at will; and so on. Reflect upon all this and then tell me if you do not believe in at least the possibility of the following scenario: In a technologically advanced country (of which there are a few), a man with the right dose of narcissism and masochism (of which there are too many) comes across scientists who would undertake any experiment, regardless of the consequences, if it helps to clarify their hypotheses (and of those, alas, there are almost as many as scientists). The result of the encounter is the pregnant male.

I will not live to see the advent of the new Androgynous Society. Perhaps it is just as well. I am one of those "men above forty" identified by Badinter as least malleable to change. In my time men often succeeded in subjugating women by the unscrupulous use of any and all means, from blarney to intimidation. And the most submissive of the women accepted all, from absurd fashion to plastic surgery. It is very unlikely that those of us who grew to become inured to this state of worldly discomfiture would adjust to the new times, when men will be asked to pay their meed in tribute to Woman's new assertiveness. Were I to be granted some form of post-death consciousness, I would not take kindly to the spectacle of my fellow males complaining of morning sickness, muscle-men flaunting protuberant abdomens, boot-camp sergeants asking for maternity leave, or my own grandson announcing that he is "with child." But I would be curious to see the state of the world and how new generations learn to cope with the new conditions. I bet that I would find the young reading the seminal documents of the founders of the Androgynous Reality, which probably would be made obligatory reading material in schools. Children would memorize some of those texts, like the closing words of Badinter's *L'Amour en Plus:* "Let us simply take note of the invincible will of women to share the universe, and the children, with men. No doubt this is going to change the future of the human condition. Whether the end of man or the rediscovery of paradise be forecasted, it shall be Eve, once again, the agent responsible for the change."[11]

ON MALE JEALOUSY

Jealousy is the most complex of the passions. Others may be looked at squarely, without interposition. But jealousy is always derivative: a passion born of another passion, like a reflection, or an echo. Note that jealousy never arises in a consciousness that is untroubled: It needs, to crystallize, the matrix of some preexisting agitation, be it love, ambition, or possessiveness. Woman's generosity, unwisely but not always in error, is willing to believe that the jealous man is a man in love. This is why many would rather see the lover irate than calm and equanimous in the face of real or assumed betrayal. "A kindness like yours hurts more than bastinades," says the adulterous woman in Marcel Pagnol's *Baker's Wife* to the outwardly calm husband who receives her in the conjugal domicile after her scandalous escapade. The strange logic has ancient roots: in Lucian's *Scenes of Courtesans*, an experienced courtesan,

Ampelis, soberly indoctrinates her young apprentice on the symptoms by which a seasoned courtesan may recognize true attachment in her man: "The man who has not been jealous, beaten his mistress, torn her clothes—he has yet to be in love." Love, apparently, gives no subtler proof than that. The rest— tears, sighs, oaths, kisses, letters, tokens, and the like—are but faint shadow and insubstantial premonition. The full fire of passion comes from jealousy. "Thus," informs Ampelis to a wide-eyed Chrysis, her apprentice, "if [he] has beaten you up, he must be jealous. You may expect a great deal. . . . "

Our pragmatic era turns a sanctimonious eye to passionate behavior. The demon of jealousy is no longer a preternatural presence from hell, but a sign of sociopathic or psychologic maladjustment. We are not likely to grant that estimable human qualities live, albeit deformed and polluted, in all passions. But wisdom does not consist in the complete suppression of all passions. Hegel recognized that nothing great was ever created without a great passion. Not because creativity issues directly from passion, but because creativity presupposes the effort to overmaster passion's chaotic energy. The pernicious energy of jealousy is not without worthy elements. The violent behavior of the jealous man, although misguided, stems at bottom from a concern for the inviolate perfection of others. The very word *jealous* (from vulgar Latin *zelosus,* more at *zeal)* implies a devotion, a "zeal" to preserve the worth of a cherished object. The sole idea to share it with others is a threat to it, since to share is to make common, and to make common is to vulgarize, to demean, or to cheapen. It is by a facile assimilation that jealousy is often identified with egoism. The jealous man is a zealot, a fanatical votary who must keep his treasured relic hidden from others: he alone is fit to worship it, he believes. His excesses and his irrationality are all too clear. But his jealousy is less the outcome of self-interest than the vehement desire to avoid a profanation.

Words like *relic, zeal, profanation,* and *worship* have a strong religious connotation. It should be recalled that the Vulgate speaks of a "jealous God." The religious fervor of past times, more innocent than ours, imagined that the Supreme Being would not suffer to see the faith of mankind split and variously allotted. Tolerance could only be weakness. A true believer, conscious of serving a jealous God, was necessarily a zealot unable to endure the existence of dogmas blatantly opposed to his own.[1] Likewise, a jealous man, once convinced that the troth given him had been betrayed, was ready to punish disloyalty with the inflexible rigor he imagined the divine might would bring down on the faithless.

It is perhaps no accident that in the history of the West, Spain had the dubious distinction of pushing these intransigent notions to a disturbing extreme. The staunchest defenders of religious orthodoxy became the epitome of hypersensitive male jealousy. Spaniards and foreigners alike agree that at a certain time in the history of ideas, men of this nation created a complex net of concepts and social conventions by which they gained a violent empire on their wives, sisters, and daughters. The concept of "honor" was developed with Byzantine sophistication. Words that are still in use were coined to denote its nuances, words that have no exact equivalent in other Western languages, such as *pundonor* and *honra.* The fastidious tendency peaked—again, probably not by fortuitous coincidence—during the Counter-Reformation. The inevitable, relentless vengeance that the outraged husband wreaks by his own hand upon the disloyal wife at the slightest breach of the prescribed code of conduct is the principal theme of countless novels, legends, stories, and theater plays of the period.

Calderón de la Barca (1600–1681), one of the greatest dramatists of the time, expounded at length on this theme. *Calderonian* has become synonymous with exorbitant susceptibility in matters of *honra*. The titles of some of his best-known plays are quite descriptive of the subject matter: *The Surgeon of His Honor; Secret Vengeance for Secret Insult; The Painter of His Own Dishonor; The Greatest Monster, Jealousy*.

Consider, for instance, a play by another dramatist of those times, *Los Comendadores de Córdoba (The Commanders of Córdoba)*. It was written by Lope de Vega (1562–1635), the greatest Spanish poet of the era and possibly the most prolific who ever lived. First printed in 1609, its theme is the horrible vengeance that a government official of Córdoba, Fernán Alonso, took on his adulterous wife, Beatriz de Hineshosa, and her relatives. The story is rigorously true. The homicide made a declaration in which the hair-raising facts were meticulously detailed, extant in historical archives, duly signed on April 22, 1471. But somehow the frightful crime tickled the national fancy, became a legend, and was made a folk narrative that appeared under various guises, one of which was used by Lope for his famous play. *The Commanders of Córdoba* is one of Lope's masterpieces. In contrast with Calderón's dramas, in which husbands punish not the consummate adultery but the merely suspected one, Lope's protagonist discovers his wife *in flagrante delicto*. The action is powerful and direct. "There is here nothing but blood and lust," wrote a prestigious critic, shocked but in admiration of the speed with which the reader is drawn into a bloody vertigo, "so unlike the intricate casuistry by which Calderonian husbands prepare their revenges." The wife in Lope's play invites her cousin-lover into her bedroom, while her lady-in-waiting does the same for the cousin's brother. As if this foursome were not enough, a servant of the seducer brothers pairs off with a maid of the disloyal women, affording Lope the opportunity to oppose comical dialogues in savory vernacular to the more polished and conventional amorous exchanges of the other two couples. While these complicated, delicately synchronized goings-on are taking place, the outraged husband returns. He had been previously alerted to the collective betrayal by the sight of his lady's ring on his rival's finger and had faked a forced absence from the homestead. He now comes back surreptitiously into his house, sword in hand. His revenge is as swift as the rest of the action. The irate avenger kills the seducer, the seducer's brother, the lady-in-waiting, the butler, the cook, two black slaves, and a monkey that was kept as a pet in the household. His wife he slays only after she comes back to her senses from a swoon provoked by the sudden sight of her husband. This slight delay is intentional: He wants her "to feel her death." She asks for confession, and the dutiful husband obliges by sending for a friar with the sole surviving servant—the only one who had the good fortune of becoming an informer for the master at the right time. After the wife takes confession, she is dispatched to the beyond as expeditiously as the rest of the victims. A parrot is discovered in its cage. The unlucky bird is slain on the spot, just like the rest of the dwellers, for the reason that "He witnessed all, and, able to talk, / His words retained." Thus, culpable like the rest, since he knew and did not tell, the unfortunate parrot is unceremoniously shipped off to an avian paradise.

We must believe that the arch-Catholic society of Seville, Madrid, or Toledo applauded with gusto every time this hideous bloodbath was represented on the stage. It seems likely that austere men of the frock, if they included the theater as one of the honest amusements by which to solace the rigor of their pious pursuits, must have nodded approvingly on the scenes of retributive butchery. In the final scene of *The Commanders of Córdoba,* the king hears the relation of the murders directly from the lips of the uxoricide, who has just accomplished the nefarious deed. In courtly, elegant verses, the monarch praises the gentleman's resolve in restoring his *honra* to its previous immaculate shine, and gives him a high-born lady of the nobility in marriage, to compensate the poor man, as it were, for his loss!

It is difficult, from our present vantage point, to consider these customs dispassionately. Honor as a sentiment that must wash off affronts with blood occurs in the literature of all nations, but its exaggeration is typically Spanish. Our deodorized, pulchritudinous times, distrustful of passion, tend to dismiss this attitude as sheer barbaric excess. In the sense that it permitted the subjugation and brutalization of women, nothing can be said in its defense. But it would be rashly unperceptive to conclude that *honra* was "nothing but" obscurantism and savagery. To do so would be to remain blind to the subtler aspects of the culture that spawned this notion and hence to one of the noblest efforts to uplift man from a purely material existence. I am reminded that Voltaire was impervious to the greatness in Shakespearean theater. "It is much to be lamented," he wrote, "that there is more barbarism than genius in his [Shakespeare's] works." The prim, refined philosopher found it incomprehensible that anyone would take delight in seeing eyes gouged and lunatics raving on the stage. That Englishmen should stomach such atrocities (and did so, without compunction, in the company of their king!) only served to reaffirm Voltaire's conclusion that the British had yet to climb a long way before attaining the civilized perfection of the Gallic race. As to the rich symbolism and insights of Shakespeare's plays, Voltaire saw nothing. Similarly, the Spanish honor plays may offend contemporary standards, but this should not make us impervious to the rich spiritual context from which the concept of *honra* accrued. It was an infirm and extravagant by-product of Spain in its "Golden Century." But Spanish civilization's main title to greatness is, and has always been, the unambiguous claim that man's life must be ruled by high ideals, by concepts that transcend him and that must supersede any consideration of convenience, practicality, or expediency. In this quest Spain has often erred, as her appalling disasters attest; but she has never compromised, as her undying glory proclaims.

Not surprisingly, "honor" so drastically understood has sparked opinions as varied as the character and temperament of the framers. To a German scholar of the turn of the century, this supererogation to honor that makes men inflict terrible punishments on the mere suspicion of a fault "is always an ideal principle, since it rests on that high moral standard that upholds principles regardless of the consequences."[2] Prejudice, envy, and vanity may wrongly avail themselves of immoderate power, "but even in these travesties we recognize the shadows of a sublime idea." More sanguine, French critics dissented from this uncritical glorification of a pernicious turn of mind, but often ascribed *honra* to a primitive and inhumane disposition of the soul. Thus Viel-Castel,[3] a French writer, denied that it was a virtue, "at least insofar as we would like to think that virtue has a Christian significance," and declared that "something of the Islamic Orient" had admixed itself with Western culture and produced collective irrationality in the Iberian peninsula. Less fractious, other erudites preferred to see Spanish *honra* as a tragedian's instrument, a sort of fate or destiny acting of its own accord, like destiny in Greek tragedies, to bring the protagonists to their inexorable, bloody end. What was *honra* to the personages of the truculent dramas themselves? Their sketchy statements seem to refer to the opinion of others. *Honra* and good reputation, or general esteem, are generally equivalent. It was not something inherent to virtuous conduct, but conferred upon the honored individual by others, especially by women. "Well you say that *honra* is in others, and not in oneself," replies the surviving servant to his revengeful master in Lope's drama, "For if your wife didn't have it, she could not have taken it away / So that who has it is not you, but who takes it away." Moreover, it is a gift of peculiar attributes: It can be increased, or removed entirely, but it cannot be diminished or partly lost. And yet, when lost, it is like losing life itself. Health, riches, and good fortune are as nothing without it. In consequence, a man must forever stand watch and do all he can to prevent its loss. But if he should lose it, he must immediately obtain revenge: This is the only effective means to restore it.

It must not be supposed, however, that this opinion was universal. Contemporary with the plays of Lope and Calderón, there were many in Spain who appealed to reason and Christian charity, and linked honor with principles higher than the opinion of others. One example is found in a charming short novel, *El Celoso Extremeño (The Jealous Man from Extremadura)*, that we owe to the genius of Cervantes. It is one of his "exemplary novels," and a true gem in the rich panoply of world letters. The plot is simple. A rich old man, Filipo de Carrizales, marries an adolescent girl and surrounds her with all manner of precautions designed to ensure her conjugal fidelity. This dream of his declining years was, as every reader anticipates, not to be. The maliciousness of a dissolute chaperone—the traditional *dueña*—and the cunningness of a rakish young suitor combine to thwart the husband's illusion of everlasting marital bliss. With the complicity of a servant, the young evildoer gains access to the forbidding fortress of a house that guards the coveted prize. Although the old man arrives to surprise the young couple asleep in each other's arms, Cervantes is respectful of the conventional morality of his times and leads the reader to understand that by a felicitous train of improbable circumstances, the girl's virtue stood unblemished. Then, in a startling departure from the obligatory bloodshed that serves as denouement to so many Spanish narratives of the period, the elderly husband unexpectedly waxes philosophical. He does not unsheath his Toledan blade: age, if not wisdom, loathes passion's radical solutions. He fathoms the arrogance that had impelled him to blindly disregard the normal course of human propensities and thus realizes his own guilt. Still more: He lets his wife know that he intends to double her inheritance upon his death "for as I was extreme in all I did, let my vengeance be likewise conformed, and exerted upon myself as *guiltiest party* to this crime." The sole condition for this liberality is that the victim must, soon after his death, marry her would-be seducer. But one week after the generous clause is inserted in the old man's testament, Providence has reimplanted the rule of justice. We find then the old man dead, the repentant wife recluse in a monastery where she intends to take her vows, the young man disillusioned and on his way to the New World (or, in another version of the novel, dead from the accidental explosion of a musket that he held in his arms), and the perfidious *dueña* utterly confounded by the undoing of her knavish schemes.

Around this simple plot, largely fashioned after the conventions of Renaissance amorous intrigue, the narrative weaves a lively pattern of engrossing observations. The jealous old man is introduced with little sympathy. He is an *indiano,* that is, a parvenu grown rich in the Indies, the newly discovered continent. Cervantes has no partiality for those who chose this shortcut to power and riches. His idea of the New World is unmistakingly unflattering: "refuge and asylum of the desperate of Spain, church of the subversive, safe-conduct of homicides . . . cover of gamblers . . . general lure of loose women, common decoy of the many and particular remedy of the few." It has even been said that Cervantes carried a chip on his shoulder concerning the American continent; that his contempt for immigrants reflected his own spite at not having been granted permission to emigrate, since his many applications for a bureaucrat's post in the New World were consistently denied. Be that as it may, Carrizales is introduced in the novel with little effort at provoking sympathy on his behalf. We, therefore, expect a clownish personage, the target of ridicule, the "old cuckold" of ancient and modern farce. Cervantes saves him from this fate by the simple expedient of granting him *a priori* jealousy. In effect, we are told that even before getting married, Filipo de Carrizales was jealous in the extreme; that merely to imagine himself wedded was enough to spark in him vehement representations of suspicion and betrayal; and that his fright was so great on those occasions that he shook uncontrollably, his composure fell to pieces, and his mind was in shambles. The old man, therefore, is no cardboard figure. He is animated by quintessential jealousy: jealousy antedating fact. Like Shakespeare, Cervantes understood this "surreal" attribute of jealousy: that it exists outside of reality and has little or no connection with objective facts as we know them. It is a self-feeding monster, with no need of "real" experience to be born, to thrive, or to die. And because Carrizales enters the novel under this tragic sign, we understand the depth of his suffering. He is a man condemned to broil in his own juices, like all victims of jealousy who ever lived—if life be the proper name for their torments.

Next, we witness his pitiful, uphill struggle to preserve his peace of mind. He surrounds the conjugal domicile with thick walls. He seals the windows, except at the top, where a patch of blue is all that is visible. He chooses female servants only; for the post of stablegroom, however, he appoints a black eunuch. This one attends to the feeding and conditioning of the horses—all mares—kept in the stables. In fact, all the animals of the household are females, just like the servants. The young wife, Leonora, once entered into her new home, never hears the song of a he-bird. Neither does she hear a dog bark: only bitches are kept. The walls are hung with tapestries that represent pious scenes from the Gospels. But even here male figures have been carefully excluded, leaving only the likenesses of saintly women, landscapes, and religious symbols. Massive doors with heavy locks segregate the courtyard and the stables from the interior of the house, where the women's bedrooms are located. The keys are kept by the master at all times. Even though the black groom is a certified eunuch, he has no access to the heavily guarded seraglio. Provisions and victuals are delivered weekly by a steward who does not come into the house; all transactions with the outside world take place in the street, according to a rigid protocol. The master of the house opens the street door only at fixed times. The delivered goods are transported by the groom to the patio and placed on a contraption that good old Carrizales had the foresight to construct. It is a swiveling device with wooden shelves, such as were then styled in convents and monasteries, on which the various articles may be placed. It is made to rotate on its vertical axis, like a revolving door, and by this means foodstuffs and merchandise gain access to the inner chamber, there to be picked up by the women. Its panels are so placed that deliverer and receiver never come within view of each other.

In reality, the whole house is a contraption, a large-scale mechanical trap designed to ensnare the unseizable determinants of marital infidelity. And the greatest absurdity is that everyone knows the uselessness of the behemoth machine. The intended prey was already inside, in the brain of the inventor, before he thought of assembling his clever trap. And, in a way, all the participants of the drama were already trapped. The popular notion is that jealousy implies an amorous "triangle," with lover, beloved, and rival, respectively, at each vertex. An intriguer enters the picture, and a "quadrangle" is formed. Yet more complex geometries are well known and fully exploited by novelists, playwrights, and regular gossips alike. But the true unfolding of the drama is always highly individual, and its development has full meaning only for one—the jealous one. Proof of this is that jealousy may run its entire course, beginning, middle, and end, without any of the participants of the drama, outside of the jealous one, becoming aware of what is happening. Carrizales recognized the fundamental solipsism of this passion when he said: "It was I who, like the silkworm, built around me the house in which I was to die." So, Carrizales's house is a concretized symbol of jealousy. Bars, locks, thick walls, and heavy doors are like mortuary swathes, which the old man wraps concentrically around himself and his women, in a prefiguration of death and burial—the "live burial" of jealousy.

The rival is often assumed to be central to the drama of jealousy, but in reality plays a very secondary role. The very existence of a rival is completely unimportant: He may be fictitious, yet the play goes on all the same. The true jealous man is always jealous *a priori*. As the accident-prone are not the unblessed victims of chance but suffer ill winds *because* they are accident-prone, so the jealous man drinks his cup of sorrows not because he has a rival but has a rival because he is jealous. He needs a rival so badly that if he did not have one he would invent him. This is why extreme jealousy sees a rival in *every* man. I was barely an adolescent when I watched a film of the late director Luis Buñuel that dealt with the Spanish obsession with this peculiar style of self-entombment, pathologic jealousy. I do not know what film critics might think today of this little-known production of the famous director, completed in two or three weeks of filming time, with a ridiculously meager budget, using actors who were either wrongly typecast or frankly inept, and under the bureaucratic duress that attended most of his career in Mexico. What I know is that Buñuel himself deemed this film, laconically entitled *Él (He)*, one of his most consummate undertakings. He felt he had succeeded in transferring his inner demons, species of which we all carry with us in greater or lesser measure, to the screen. The surfeit of the demons' maliciousness defies description: They torture the jealous man by transforming every trivial aspect of daily life into a cause for suspicion. The recondite recesses of hell could have spawned no more exquisite torture than this universal falsification of reality. If she turns the patio's lights on, is this a signal to a forewarned lover, privy to the preconcerted sign? If her behavior is demure and irreproachable, is she trying to lull the husband into a false sense of security, only to more fully indulge her lustfulness when his vigilance slackens? In a scene of Luis Buñuel's film, the jealous man, in his wife's bedroom, pushes a long needle through the door's keyhole, in a cruel and absurd aggression against a man who—the husband imagines—may be watching through the opening.

In spite of the convenient textbook criteria that specialists set forth, the distinction between the madman and the jealous man is a difficult one. The madman, like the man in love, the jealous man, or the man prey to any overwhelming passion, is "a patient," that is, a passive agent in the grip of a force that seems to be outside himself. Madman and passionate man are both tossed in piteous agitation, immersed in delirium, or plunged into unwholesome reveries. Both derive the greatest harm from an inalterable incapacity to exert self-control. We know too little of the organic determinants of pathologic mental states, but I would wager that when these become clarified to molecular detail, the disturbance will be shown to be the same in paranoia and in the fits of jealousy. Where does jealousy end and paranoia begin? Buñuel was dismayed at the reactions of the public, which received his film with guffaws of laughter, but those scenes were not simply samples of Buñuel's notorious eccentricity. Passion *does* bring about madness, albeit usually in transitory or intermittent attacks. The film director tells us in his memoirs an intimate detail of a neighbor of his, a respected member of the armed forces, a man whose conduct merited in every way the unreserved approbation of society. He was, however, immoderately jealous. From trustworthy witnesses, Buñuel found out that this man had once faked a business trip, returned to his house in the early hours of the morning, knocked at the door of his own house, and said in a simulated voice that his wife, a woman of irreproachable conduct, could not identify: "Mary, let me in. Now that your husband is away, let's profit from the opportunity. . . ."

Jealousy is self-limiting madness, like all passions. But there is a point of no return: It merges into paranoia when certainty displaces the capacity to doubt. Here lies still one more paradox. The jealous man may be said to be sane for as long as he is able to pass his doubts in review, to question some of his own premises, and in lucid moments, to suspend his judgments. But the moment arrives when he is no longer capable of calling forth such representations as would cast a doubt on all his suspicions. The abolition of his freedom to judge critically ushers in the advent of mental illness. It is the complete triumph of intellectual consciousness over passionate consciousness that signifies madness. Doubt is the chief torture of the jealous man who remains sane. He desires to know but at the same time fears intensely the knowledge that he seeks. True jealousy never stems from the absolute certainty that one is deceived, but from suspecting the possibility of deceit. "Does she love someone else?" "Perhaps she is not the one I thought she was. . . ."

This suspicion is, of course, demeaning to the love object. Therefore, it contradicts the "zeal" inherent in jealousy, by which the jealous lover wishes to maintain the value of the love object and defend it against threats of degradation. We would not expect passion to be free of contradiction. But how more degrading is to the jealous man the confirmation of his suspicions! And yet, confirmation is what he seeks frantically, relentlessly. Othello screams to Iago:

Villain, be sure thou prove my love a whore!
Be sure of it; give me the ocular proof.

And with equally unswerving fervor, he presses for valid, irrefutable evidence:

Make me to see't; or at least so prove it
That the probation bear no hinge nor loop
To hang a doubt on—or woe upon thy life!
                    (Shakespeare, *Othello* Act III, sc. iii, 365ff.)

Thus, when the obsession becomes pathologic we recognize its pathologic character by features other than irrationality; the concatenation of ideas is only *too* rational, and the vehement desire for valid, testable truth would be envied by the most rationalist philosopher. A jealous man who goes mad no longer doubts: in a way, he is craziest when he is at his most rational. Until then, he had been the toy of that dialectical oscillation that bounced him between doubt and certainty. This is the mark of sanity. But now that he no longer doubts, he is distinguishable from simply passionate men by one other mark: that whereas the passionate may heal of themselves, the cure of the mad must be entrusted to others. The madman is he who must be healed by third parties.

Jealousy moves equally to pity and to laughter. It is telling of our uncharitableness that the suspicious husband has furnished material for comedy from time immemorial. The crowd's undiscerning peals of laughter during the showing of Buñuel's film have stood in my memory for decades; and the discrepancy between the harrowing scenes, the squalor and the pathos of the situation, and the mirthful reaction of a large segment of the public continues to puzzle me. It may be that certain peoples, more prone to emphasize the notion of honor, are also less disposed to tolerance of human foibles and castigate with ridicule the slighting of prevailing mores. I confess to having been influenced by cultural conditioning and to having taken unkindly to representation of the idea of the "complacent husband." In my younger years, the inexhaustible theme of

French narratives never amused me. This is the infinite variations, fictional and historical, of the "understanding" husband who surprises his wife in the midst of the unconscionable frolic with a lover, and cautiously closing the door of the bedroom into which he had unwittingly intruded, admonishes: "Madame, please! You must be more careful. What if, instead of me, someone else had opened the door?" Not that I looked with favor upon automatic knifing under the circumstances described, but nurtured as I was in Calderón and Lope, the logic of the admonition completely escaped me.

Equally puzzling is agreement over the cast and shape of this ridicule. At least all Mediterranean peoples seem to concur that the stigma of a deceived husband is frontal and keratinous: He manifests his betrayal by growing horns. A thorough investigation of the origin of this myth is still to be written. It seems improbable that the Italy of the Renaissance, notwithstanding its vast and fertile plains of cuckoldom, would have originated the peculiar myth. If it had been so, Michelangelo would never have come up with the idea of placing horns atop the lionesque mane of his celebrated *Moses*. Exodus 34:29 would imply that they were shafts of light, but we recognize horns when we see them.[4] Would Sigmund Freud, to whom we owe no less than an erotic interpretation of the universe, have let go the opportunity to unveil the subtle rapport between the prophet's appendages and the betrayed condition? Freud, in his extensive essay on the famous statue, remains silent on this point. He comments at length on the position of the prophet's fingers, the inclination of his head, and so forth, but nowhere does he suggest that horns had anything to do with broken pledges. Mind you, he concludes that Moses is about to blast the faithless Israelites who continued to adhere to the idolatrous worship of the golden calf, but in spite of that he eschews any mention of a relation between apostasy and the cornual state. All of which renders it likely that Freud's Vienna, too, ignored the hypothesis that a connection exists between disloyalty and frontal excrescence.

Full elucidation of the origins of the myth would require no small a research effort, and greater mastery of philology than I can summon. Think, for now, of this myth's evocative power. If women's disloyalty is granted the ability to raise horns on the pledge holder's forehead, would their misconduct show a close correspondence with the induced effects? For example, would a simple flirt bring about mere "pointing" or the small, velvety protrusions of a young calf? Would a wife's arrant promiscuity bring about the broad and ramifying antlers of a caribou? Would her philandering, when mixed with intrigue and scheming, result in the retroflexed, incurved ram's horns? If so, a classification of the heterogeneous species of cuckoldry would at last be possible, thus contributing to the advancement of science. No doubt we would learn to distinguish between husbands to whom horns are useful organs in the biologic struggle, others for whom they are a deleterious encumbrance destined to disappear in evolution, and still others who periodically lose and renew their forehead's equipment, just like some ruminants.

One shudders to think of the unfortunate coincidences that this myth made possible. The growth of keratinous processes on the skin of human beings is an uncommon but well-known disease. It was noted by Morgagni in the seventeenth century, who thought that those affected somehow partook of the nature of ruminants. The technical name of the disease is *cornu cutaneum,* or cutaneous horn. To be precise, it is not a specific disease, but a syndrome. A keratinous excrescence may grow out of various pathologic skin processes, from benign cysts that discharge keratinous contents to the exterior, to skin cancers overlaid by exuberant keratin production from the superficial epidermis. The result is the same: a dense, brownish, horn-like protrusion emerges from the skin. When the height of the excrescence is at least three times the diameter of its base, say contemporary dermatologists, the lesion has earned the name of cutaneous horn. An apposite designation: The resemblance to an animal's horn is striking. The lesion is usually very small, but years ago a medical publication illustrated a spectacular case of a cutaneous horn that had grown on the forehead—an uncommon location—of a patient who had opted to leave it untreated for years. The result was dramatic. The excrescence had grown, broadened, incurved, and come to resemble a ram's horn, utterly disfiguring the unfortunate man's facial appearance.

Imagine the unhappy occurrence in a country where the link between cornuateness and cuckoldry is deeply ingrained in the collective mind. The situation would be as laughable as it would be dramatic. Achille Campanile has made this hypothetical event the theme of one of his humorous novels.[5] A young wife, returning from a short vacation in the countryside, where the husband was unable to join her, finds him afflicted by frontal cutaneous horn of recent development. A glance to his forehead, and she faints. No sooner has she recovered her senses and seen her husband again than she confesses that she has been unfaithful. It is impossible to soften the impact of this confession. The wife's mother is among those who try in vain to make her recant. The older lady has persuasion and dialectic argumentation of the first order. She tells her daughter: "Your fatal mistake was to confuse a metaphor with reality. Horns are a disease. There is no relationship between infidelity and this form of pathology. Horns would have grown on your husband's forehead even if you had remained perfectly faithful." But it is difficult to convince anyone that the relationship is a fallacy when centuries of conspicuous national folklore have driven this idea, that horns and marital infidelity are linked, deep into the subconscious. The young adultress cannot help wondering, "What if there was a connection?" She asks: "At what time did my husband have the first symptoms?" And upon hearing the answer, she is fully persuaded that her actions are the etiology of the disease: the timing of her husband's early symptoms coincides with the temporal occurrence of her moral failing.

A stern moralist might condemn this humor. To make the plight of others an occasion for mirth is uncharitable and unfeeling. But spontaneous laughter is rarely reprehensible. In a world where causes of gloom and dejection are never in shortage, to find fit reasons to laugh should be one earnest, universal concern. And then, it is not excluded that the victims of laughter, the scorned men themselves, may find that they, too, can draw from the large repository of humor that is made available. I remember a jealous man who had overcome the worst stages of his jealousy and referred to his past torments with the freedom and elation of one who has just escaped disaster unscathed. "In the worst of the crisis I thought I would kill her," he said. Then he added: "I realized I didn't even have a weapon. I looked at myself in the mirror, and saw a ridiculous 'horned' man. How was I going to kill her? By goring, perhaps?"

I place great faith in man's ability to overcome his limitations. I believe he will free himself, one day, of the pernicious rule of jealousy. Would that laughter be a part of his future therapy! The Stoic philosophers taught that the virtuous man should approach the monster of jealousy with the same raw courage that helps him to confront other passions; that he should come boldly to its presence until he can feel its fetid breath, and then say, with commanding voice strengthened by the resolve never to be the bond-slave of hell: "Lie down and sleep!" The method was never known to work. Today, some dream that medical white knights, armed cap-a-pie with syringes and electrodes, will approach the treacherous, cruel monster; and that, as it holds back its snake-wreathed head, girt with black clouds, fire, and smoke, the white knights will smite it dead with combined thrusts of analeptics and narco-leptics—right in the hypothalamus. There is no reason to doubt that this method may work. But it must be remembered that the proper goal is not to annihilate passion, but to tame it and put it to our service. I do not know what strategies man's cunning craft will develop to accomplish this heroic deed. I have no idea with what armed forces the ruthless enemy will be pressed or with what attendant trains war will be waged on him. But I hope laughter will be one of them. For all passions, by excluding the capacity to judge, become rigid mechanisms; and mechanical rigidity is, as Bergson pointed out, the very stuff of comedy. My dream is that future ther-apists will teach jealous persons to laugh at themselves with a laughter that says: "So, that is all it was!" Let then the monster come forth and fix us with its spiteful green eyes, framed by the thick, shaggy mane of writhing serpents that lick its face. It will run away, its tail between its legs, the moment it hears us laugh.

THE REMEDIES OF LOVE

> *L'amant trahi par ce qu'il aime*
> *Veut-il guérir presque en un jour?*
> *Qu'il aime ailleurs; l'amour lui-même*
> *Est le remède de l'amour.*[1]
>
> Marivaux

There is an old and unverifiable tradition in the history of Western medicine that credits Praxagoras of Cos with the discovery of the pulse in the fourth century B.C. This important discovery, however, was overshadowed by an empirical observation that kept clinicians of the ancient world agog: that the pulse may serve as an indicator—or as we would say today, "a useful diagnostic sign"—of the love passion. Ancient chroniclers, starting with Valerius Maximus, are unanimous in attributing this finding to Erasistratus, famous physician of Alexandria, and first to realize that love and pulse throb in unison, so to speak. The "juiciest" narrators of this episode in the history of medicine are Plutarch, in his *Life of Demetrius,* and Lucian, in *Syrian Gods.* The respective stories vary considerably in the details, which shows that accuracy was probably the least pressing concern of ancient historians, a happy cast of mind that, to my eye, recommends them highly.

At any rate, the story goes as follows: A young prince, Antiochus, had fallen madly in love with his stepmother, Stratonice. Knowing that this sentiment was as shameful as it was unlawful, he tried to hide the culpable passion. At length, remorseful and tormented, he resolved to die by refusing all food. His strength left him, and his body was gradually drained of vigor and substance, but the cause of the illness remained unnoticed. Erasistratus was consulted, and he observed that every time that Stratonice came to visit the patient, this one fell prey to physiological turmoil: The young man broke out in a sweat, his voice faltered, his limbs trembled, and his face flushed. Most remarkable were alterations in the rate and quality of the pulse, which became "now lively, now slothful" *(modo vegetore, modo languidore)*. Erasistratus refined his diagnosis by resorting to what has become the obligatory test for clinical investigation. When the suspected cause of the disorder was removed, the patient improved; when new exposure was deliberately provoked, a recrudescence of the symptoms always followed. Thus, as soon as Stratonice left the bedside, the young man's pulse resumed its normal rhythm, and the labored respirations disappeared. And when Antiochus's father, Seleucos, came alone to visit, or when women other than Stratonice appeared in the room, the symptomatology was never reproduced.

Once confirmed in his certainty, the astute clinician was ready to disclose his findings. This he did, but to his honor it must be said that he had first outlined a treatment for this malady, if malady it be. Discreetly drawing Seleucos aside, Erasistratus gravely announced that the cause of the illness was without remedy. None was possible, he said, because Antiochus had fallen desperately in love with his own—Erasistratus's—wife. Upon hearing the startling news, the dejected father begged the physician to procure the means to alleviate the young man's plight; in other words, to bring the woman and let her, in a manner of speaking, be the medicine. "How would you like," retorted the sharp physician, "to find yourself in my predicament, having to choose between dishonor as a husband or as a professional?" The tearful father then remonstrated, in the most heartrending accent, that the preservation of life was the highest duty, especially for a physician. With moving expressions and pathetic appeals, he added that no measure would seem dishonorable to him if it could rescue his dear son from death, a certain issue if nothing was done. Erasistratus answered: "In that case, the cure is entirely in your hands; you are the husband, the father, the king, and you can be the proper physician for your own family." A word to the wise. Seleucos understood, summoned a general assembly of his people, and announced that henceforth he was appointing his son Antiochus as king of Upper Asia, with Stratonice as his queen.

Modern historians no longer take kindly to the romantic stories of ancient Greek and Roman novelists. In this early episode of unilateral wife-swapping between father and son, they see a transfer of power prompted by political, not sentimental, reasons. Some have suggested that Seleucos had in mind to institute some form of co-regency even at the time he took Stratonice as his bride. The piquant elements of this otherwise entertaining "soap opera" are utterly disregarded. Our concern, however, is not with the historicity of the incident. We wish to illustrate only the pathophysiology of the erotic, although this phrase has a ring disturbingly suspicious of a tautology.

It seems certain that the feat of diagnostic acumen achieved by Erasistratus made quite a splash in medical circles at that time. As everyone knows, fashion is not alien to medicine. This may be why the notion became widely accepted that a specifically erotic quality of the pulse permitted the diagnosis of the amorous passion. The devil only knows what embroilments may have been caused by this unscientific presumption of the doctors of that era! The fact is, medicine had to wait for the advent of Hippocrates before this pernicious fallacy was discarded. For Hippocrates himself lay it to rest. No such "erotic pulse" exists, said he; the pulse is a clinical sign that has no specificity, and arteries pulsate irregularly under varied causes. Nevertheless, love is one of these causes. And he proceeded to illustrate the usefulness of keen observation of bodily signs in the diagnosis of erotic love, precisely by diagnosing this disorder in a fresh case. A woman passed her nights unable to sleep, refused all food, seemed distraught, and displayed profound changes of mood without apparent cause. But Hippocrates noted that when the name of a male dancer of those times, Pylades,[2] was pronounced in her presence, a complex group of somatic changes was triggered: cutaneous vasodilatation, quickening of the pulse, and a change of outward expression (Hippocrates' undying fame is due, it will be recalled, to his fine descriptions of "facies" in disease, among other brilliant observations). And, as in the case of the patient studied by Erasistratus, confirmatory maneuvers brought forth the anticipated results; in other words, reiteration of the stimulus reproduced the symptoms every time, whereas the names of other men—pronounced by the clinical investigator in the presence of the patient under carefully matched circumstances—had no detectable effect.

It is easy to see how this syndrome had to become a problem

for nosology. Could it be called a disease? Yes, since the patient obviously suffers. No, since it could not be called "contrary to nature," as required in early definitions. Yes, since the sufferer is clearly in pain. No, since the intervention of the physician is not really necessary. Yes, since the condition is potentially fatal. No, since it can cure of its own accord or by the satisfaction of a normal desire, as stated by the commonplace, "love is its own physician." This debate lasted for centuries and, like so many others, never really did receive a satisfactory resolution. Exhausted debaters simply ceased asking the question, and the question eventually lost relevance when all the terms of its formulation had changed. But as to the severity of the external manifestations of the disorder, no one doubted the rather frightening proportions. For in its most violent form, the love passion hits the victim with considerable impact. Reason is beclouded, the senses perturbed, and the imagination distorted. The lovelorn individual thinks of nothing if it does not touch his (or her) idol; and his monomania is amply reflected in the reiterative nature of his discourse. Mark the objective signs, as intense as the symptoms: pallor, lack of appetite, loss of weight, lassitude, sunken or reddened eyes with circular shadows about them, fear of accustomed routines, and tendency to seek solitary seclusion, there to brood and sigh. Pity this victim of love: All is lost for him, for he is fallen, prostrated, utterly without resources, divided between hope and fear, one minute buoyant, the next despairing; his heart has become a troubled sensor of the tempestuous commotions, and it beats now languorous, now quickened at the sight or at the mere mention of the object of his passion.

The worst feature of this disorder is that it is without remedy. At most, one can hope to extirpate it in the bud, before its roots grow deep and it becomes ineradicable. This was the conclusion at which the sages arrived. "Utterly hotheaded and reckless; as a man who would do a somersault into a ring of knives; as one who would jump into fire." So did Socrates speak of Critobolus when he heard that his disciple had kissed a youth of great beauty. The wise should keep their distance from the fair; for lovers were called "archers," seeing that their glances, like arrows, can hurt from afar. From Ovid on down, the admonition of the prudent is to avoid all sight and frequentation of the potential source of passion. And the stern Christian moralists enjoined us to vividly represent in our minds the perilous risk that erotic passion poses to our conscience, to our honor, to our estate, and more generally to our peace of mind. All to no avail. In sensitive dispositions, the slightest exposure suffices to kindle the conflagration. One glance, and the dart sinks into the target; and wherever the lover goes, the spear goes with him, as the arrow stays with the wounded deer, the feathered butt protruding from its flank, while point and shaft sink with each motion.

Short of permanent and complete absence of exposure, there is no way to thwart the progress of the ailment. Naïve were the ancient moralists who tried to give us practical rules to contain the spreading fire. Listen to their prescriptions: Those in imminent danger of engulfment by erotic passion must keep their minds constantly occupied by lofty thoughts, and their imagination filled with examples of the purest virtue; they must seek the company of the modest, the temperate, and the righteous; for by assiduous contact with probity and goodness they shall be freed of lascivious thoughts and idle daydreaming. Alas, as if youth had ever been receptive to such dissuasion when the promptings of love had once been felt! To judge from the accumulated casualties of past ages, legions assumed cured in theory were left to writhe, squirm, and agonize in practice. The not-so-young were naturally supposed to possess more effective safeguards in weighty preoccupations, such as affairs of state, financial dealings, or the pursuit of momentous projects capable of touching the lives of millions. Alas, once more: Caesar at one and the same time pursued Cleopatra and the aggrandizement of the empire, just as Louis XIV simultaneously planned his strategy in the battlefields of Europe and in the bedrooms of La Vallière, Montespan, and others. Recurrent news of scandals in the highest circles of government of virtually all countries is proof that the list has not ended of statesmen who hesitate between lickerishness and dutiful government. One shudders to think, when the two come in conflict, which one is most apt to be chosen by those to whom is entrusted the destiny of nations.

One of the oldest prescriptions against this ill may be called "systematic denigration" of the love object. Ovid illustrates it with quaint empiricism in "The Remedies for Love" (lines 314–349): "If she's slender, [call her] thin as a rail; if she's dark, black as the ace of spades. If she has city ways, label her stuck-up and bitchy; if simple and good, call her a hick from the farm." In other words, if you wish to free yourself from the noose that the sweet thing has looped around your neck, think of the defects of that person. No doubt you esteem your beloved above all imperfection, but if you reflect ever so slightly, you will discover some flaw: no creature born of woman is without one. Next, having identified the shortcomings, concentrate on them, exert yourself to see them with the eye of the mind in the most glaring light. Then magnify them beyond proportion and deepen a lively reflection on the defects you have discovered. Are her teeth slightly uneven? Think of her as some edentulous hag. Is her complexion spotted by a birthmark? Imagine how it would look with a magnifying glass: a horrid, warty verrucosity. Moreover, spur your inventiveness to contrive situations in which her imperfections might stand most conspicuously displayed. Is there something irritating to you in the way she laughs? Do tell her jokes often, and take her with you to watch the most hilarious comedies. Does she seem to lack grace when she treads on uneven terrain? Make sure she comes hiking with you on some rocky cliff.

That so much therapeutic ingeniosity was summoned shows that remedies were generally ineffective. Christianity was sure to look upon with disfavor the prescription that recommends a systematic disparagement of the love object. Surely, nothing can be more uncharitable than a man striving to transmute a woman into a repository of all manner of uncomeliness and repulsive attributes. To say nothing of the arrogance of such a man, for it is usually from a position of real or assumed superiority that one presumes to pass in review the defects of others. Nevertheless, Christian moralists leniently tolerated this prescription, on the premise that all is acceptable that diminishes a grievous and potentially fatal ill. "My scruples I would gladly part with," declared a man of the cloth, "if by these means men freed themselves of the lasciviousness. But the chief objection that I raise to this method is that it simply does not work." Indeed, it is weak medicine that proposes aspirin tablets for a brain tumor, or a Band-Aid for abdominal trauma with aortic transection; these parallels are not inappropriate, considering the virulence of some of the attacks. A story of the sixteenth century, before mores were mollified by the more temperate customs that rule all commerce between the sexes today, illustrates this point.

A powerful aristocrat at the court of Brussels fell in love with the daughter of a burgher of that town. He sought every occasion to meet her and to speak with her alone, that he might represent to her the intense passion that he experienced. The conservative social customs then prevailing stood in his way. Young girls found virtually no occasion to leave their homes upchaperoned. Our man pined away, spying every opportunity, only to be frustrated every time. After months of languishing in this expectant state, he approached the girl's mother, but was rebuked once more. The staid matron distrusted, not without reason, the designs that powerful men formed on girls of lower social class. The suitor was like a madman. At last, he conceived a desperate plan. He implored the mother to be permitted to speak alone to the young girl, only for as long as he could hold a live ember in his unprotected hand. Pressured by sympathetic listeners, the mother consented, convinced that the interview would have to be brief. Much to her horror and dismay, the wooer stood the test until the live coal had charred his palm to the bones. At last, the horrified mother had to interrupt the torture. It is against the overpowering effect of this emotion that moralists of past centuries opposed the childish exercise of a mental inventory of personal defects, aimed at lowering the esteem of the love object. Assuming a hypothetical lover were found with the minimum of sanity required to discern defects in the beloved, it seems hardly possible that so weak a construction could dam up the rushing torrent.

Against this background, it is not surprising that efforts to devise a cure or a vaccine should have been unrelenting. But human inventiveness, so admirable in other departments, avers itself impotent to correct the pernicious disorder. Not that traditional remedies for other bodily disorders were not tried. Every cure effective against fevers, colics, congestions, and distempers was systematically applied: tonics, decongestants, revivers, laxatives, rubefacients, restoratives, sinapisms, poultices, and balsams; all were tried, and all in vain.

Sound medical advice came from medieval doctors. A summary of their methods may be found in Rabelais's work. In Book 3 of *Pantagruel,* the physician Rondibilis discusses five methods by which too strong an erotic urge may be counteracted. The first one is to take wine immoderately. When well into his cups, all a man wishes to do is to sleep. "Bacchus, the god of drunkards, is commonly represented without his beard and in the costume of a woman, as though he were utterly effeminate, like a deballed eunuch." The caveat is that one must be perpetually semi-stuporous, for when wine is taken in moderation it elicits precisely the effect one is trying to suppress. Moderate eating and drinking abet the erotic function, or as Terence puts it, "without Ceres and Bacchus, Venus catches cold" *(Sine Cerere et Libero friget Venus)* (Eunuchas IV, 5). The second method is pharmacologic. The following plants and drugs are said by Rondibilis to render a man chilled and completely impotent for the tasks of love: The *Nymphaea heraclia,* or pond lily; the Amerine willow (a species of willow so named because it is found in Ameria, in Umbria); hempseed; the periclymenos, or honeysuckle; the vitex, or chaste tree; the mandragora; the hemlock; the smaller orchid; the hippopotamus skin; and other exotic preparations difficult to procure. A third line of defense is found in strenuous and constant physical exercise: "So it is that Diana, who is constantly occupied in the hunt, is called the chaste." Cupid, apparently, finds it hard to shoot his arrows when the target is constantly moving about. The fourth means is ardent study, for during this activity the animal spirits are so dissolved and consumed by intellectual pursuits that none are left for any other; "and the cavernous nerve, the function of which is to project these spirits outward for the propagation of human-kind, remains unfulfilled." Philosophers kept repeating that idleness is the mother of lust, and that to occupy one's mind works wonders in staving off amorous ardor. Few of them benefited from the method, and most men were left to lament its variably disappointing results. Its description by Rabelais, however, left us one of the most splendid praises of the con-templative life.

The fifth and last remedy is the venereal act. Panurge is prompt to reply: "I was waiting for that. I'll take *it* for mine." Satiety carried to surfeit produces disgust. Therefore, do it twenty-five to thirty times a day, and it will not occur to you to do it again. The method, of course, requires a cooperative partner, which is its chief limitation. As to the general effec-tiveness of this technique when it is possible to apply it, the common experience has been that it is not trustworthy. In our day, some continue to apply the method under well-defined circumstances. A female reader of the syndicated column of "Dear Abby" wrote to the famous columnist-counselor that she subjected her husband to this treatment with view to achieve prophylaxis: She arranged for a generous overdose of erotic activity every time that her husband was about to go on a business trip. She hoped, evidently, to leave him in a refractory condition for potential stimuli that might arise away from home. The correspondence of many readers in reaction to this unoriginal remedy was uniformly skeptical. Wrote a corre-spondent: "At dinner, I have sometimes gorged myself with sweets, pies, and delicacies. I find that eight hours later I am hungry again."

In more recent history, bloodletting, the universal cure of old times, did claim some reports of success, but these were sporadic and anecdotal. The prince of Condé, for instance, while madly in love with Mademoiselle Vigean, contracted an illness for which physicians prescribed liberal bleeding. In their zeal to achieve a cure, the doctors brought their illustrious patient to the very brink of complete exsanguination. Yet nature's strength prevailed over medical folly, and Condé made a miraculous recovery in spite of medical care. Much to his surprise, upon regaining bodily strength he found that his mind was no longer troubled by the former obsession. The approach of the beautiful lady Vigean he now regarded with complete indifference. This observation convinced the patient that blood was the seat of the amorous passion. A medical profession less discerning than today's was much swayed by incidents of this nature. The active principle of love circulates as an ingredient of blood: drain the latter, and with it you shall extract your infatuation.

In contrast with these rare reports, there stood myriads of individuals whose obsession continued unperturbed by severe blood loss. Throughout the protracted historical period in which duels were the accepted manner of solving amorous imbroglios, much blood was shed without reducing the intensity of the emotions that had prompted the violence. Many a defeated duelist was seen to go in and out of hemorrhagic shock uttering with the same fervid enthusiasm the name of the belle who had brought him to that difficult pass. A gentleman of those days burned in an unwholesome passion for a lady graced with many adornments, of which constancy was not one. Tired of the monotonous insistence of the lover's homage, she opted to transfer the bestowing of her favors elsewhere, to a recipient who, free from the monomaniac obsession, appeared naturally more interesting (and was probably less deserving). The first suitor was crushed: consumed, red-eyed and unkempt, he appeared before the woman, imploring her to reconsider. When it was clear that his appeals would not move her, he turned to heroic measures. Kneeling before the pitiless lady, he unsheathed his sword, placed it in her hands, and asked of her to kill him, saying that he deemed it preferable to die by her hand than to continue a life bereft of her love, for this would be tantamount to a slow agony, many times more cruel than the wound inflicted by the steel in her delicate fist.

Few would doubt that so utter a man's surrender to the empire of his mistress would unfailingly evoke those tender feelings that tradition ascribes more insistently to the female than to the male of our species. But there is no predicting the shape of a human heart's recondite impulses. The lady of our narrative, stirred by the man's harangue, thrust not one but two passes with the sword, leaving the disabused lothario at her feet, uncannily resembling a garden bug pinned to an entomologist's collection pad. The ancient chronicler says that the man lost much blood but did not die. Marvelous to recount, after a long convalescence he emerged completely cured of his former obsession. He showed, in fact, no disposition at all to renew the abruptly interrupted courtship. If now I were entrusted the task of framing these observations in the cautious terminology of the modern physician, I would state, first, that bloodletting, under carefully specified conditions, has been known to have anti-amorous effects in isolated instances. I might add that this felicitous reaction appears to depend on an interplay of ill-understood factors relating to bloodletter and -lettee. Moreover, these factors are currently obscure and therefore difficult to control, therefore making this therapy an inordinately hazardous one. I would say that further studies are needed before its value in our therapeutic armamentarium can be defined.

To grave illnesses, drastic remedies: This dictum often inspired the search for effective countermeasures. As it appeared that the sufferers were mesmerized, or under a spell or incantation, it naturally occurred to would-be therapists that a violent jolt might restore the patients to their senses. This line of reasoning was not entirely unfounded. On purely theoretical grounds, the earliest moralists had maintained that passions in full effervescence are easier to supplant than to suppress. True, lust in full swing is difficult to moderate by reason: Try and convince the rutting male that abstinence is preferable. But observation shows that passions are interchangeable: One holds sway until another one, more compelling and preponderant, forces it out and takes its place. For instance, anger may be replaced by sadness, and joy by fright. Hence, if one cannot cool off the sexually excited by mere persuasion, their ardor is sure to be diminished by scaring them out of their wits.

Here, practical observation came to the aid of theory. For many reported that they had wasted away under the wounds of love until a sudden shock or commotion had disturbed the condition in which they faded. Of a romantic poetaster, it was said that he languished under the effects of amorous obsession, eating poorly and choosing wild and stormy places to compose his passionate sonnets. The choice of landscape was quite appropriate considering the aesthetic intent; climatically, it was ill advised. In that desolate wilderness, lightning struck only a few feet away from the inspired rhymester, who fell to the ground stunned by the tremendous discharge. After he recovered he manifested the former inclination for meter and rhyme, but none for the subject that had once inspired them. Of the beauty to whom he had sworn undying fealty in high-sounding alexandrines, he scarcely remembered the name. In like manner, a famous Spanish mystic of the Middle Ages is said to have instantaneously forsaken his impetuous yearning for a woman, following a single shocking experience. The man had been a philanderer before he was uplifted by the gift of divine grace. He had pressed the pursuit of a woman to extremes that only exasperated carnal desire is known to incur. The indecorous courtship ended when the lady, despairing of being harassed, uncovered one of her breasts, on which a large, oozing ulcer was present, to the horrified sight of her suitor. From this moment on, the life of the man changed. His frivolous pursuits were abandoned, and thenceforth his thoughts were all for the salvation of his soul.

Having established the effectiveness of "shock therapy," the problem confronted by ancient therapists was how to apply the technique regularly and systematically. They needed what we would call today a "controlled environment." Legend has it that they came up with a solution, creating a sort of national reference center for the treatment of amorous passion. Its location was in Leucas (modern Greek *Levkás,* local *Levkadhia*), an island in the Ionian sea that was called Santa Maura by the Venetians (who dominated the island for a time, as did the Turks). The Greek name comes from the white cliffs of limestone that rise from its soil along the seacoast, particularly on the northeastern corner of this island. Here, the rocky elevations soar to awesome heights above the seawaters. In trials by ordeal, suspected criminals were thrown from the summit of the highest cliff, where the rocky mass advances into the sea. The famous "Leucadian leap" came to be known also as "lover's leap" because lovers desirous to cure themselves of their obsession submitted to this harsh test voluntarily, convinced that whoever underwent the shock of the experience and lived to tell about it would be freed from the shackles of love. The ceremonial cure lacked not in dramatic trappings. Imagine the despondent lover, already in a state not far removed from delirium, coming to this eerie place. The waves explode in white spume that flies asunder as the water crashes at the foot of the cliff. The solitude of the place, the distant roar of the ocean, and the acute cry of the sea gulls frame the imposing, bare, massive rock that shoots upward, hundreds of feet above the sea. From below, the summit cannot be distinguished, as it is girded by the clouds. And from the top, with a force of vertigo, the steep declivity pulls straight down, past the level at which the sea gulls inscribe their orbits, and into the cold, dark, tumultuous waters.

Many, it is said, attempted the drastic cure. Some who were obscure persons, others who had achieved renown. The poet Nicosistratus took the jump in order to forget his mistress; Artemis, queen of Caria, to forget her lover; the lesbian Sappho to forget either a lover or a mistress; and Charinus leaped to take his mind off a eunuch at the service of the Syrian king. Thus, the etiology of the ailment could be man, woman, or points in between; the treatment still worked. Had this not been so, it would be difficult to explain why a man named Maces was said to have taken the leap four times in a row. But then, again, patients are known to develop all sorts of bizarre dependencies.

In the eighteenth century, a Spanish Benedictine friar discoursing on "The Remedies Of Love" reviewed the existing literature on the subject. To this reviewer I owe many of the "case reports" described in the present chapter.[3] But after going through the acccumulated experience, he declared all remedies without efficacy. No better than placebos, he implied. In his learned examination of the "Leucadian leap" he informs us that most jumpers reached the water dead or died from the impact, much in spite of what the ancient chronicles affirmed. For it was the custom to attach many feathers and even live birds to the bodies of leapers, with the idea to mitigate the violence of their fall.[4] And with the partiality for scientific reasoning that suffused the Age of the Enlightenment, our Benedictine demonstrates that birds thus tied to falling bodies would have been impeded to take flight and would have actually accelerated the speed of the fall. Then, the most reverend father is ready to report his own, original remedy.

The first thing he does is to expound an admirable theory of the role of imagination on bodily reactions. Anticipating the work of Pavlov by more than a hundred years, he remarks that bodily reactions (pleasant or unpleasant) may be consistently associated with various interrelated stimuli; and that, in due time, the presentation of a single stimulus may suffice to trigger the whole set of reactions originally elicited by combined or associated stimuli. "Therefore, what the lovesick person must do, if he or she wishes to be cured, is, first, to select a terrible, pitiable, or otherwise moving object of negative affective content. Let it be whatever experience shows to be the most apt to shake the animus of the patient in the highest degree. Second, to become skillful in associating the idea of this object with that of the love object. This is done by transferring thoughts from this object to that one, and vice versa. This exercise need not be repeated excessively; a dozen or so times, and it will be learned thoroughly. Sometimes, with just a few repetitions the student will succeed in never being able to think of the beloved without imagining, at the same time, an object pitiable or terrible."

This is, in a nutshell, the theory developed by the good Benedictine. Scholars seem not to have realized how keenly penetrating he was. Without the help of modern theories of psychology, this perceptive student of human nature was able to develop a sophisticated mental strategy, skillfully supported by his anticipation of the modern concept of "association of ideas." But one thing is to tip our hats off to the little-recognized precursor of contemporary psychological theories, and quite another to assent to the efficacy of his recommended treatment.

The good friar leaves the choice of frightening, pitiable, or terrible object to the individual patient. He is too good a psychologist to believe in standardized therapies; he knows that the same thing will evoke pathetic emotions in one and remain a matter of indifference in another. But he yields to the temptation of presenting a detailed example of a technique that (without his saying so) I suspect he may have used himself. If for no other reason than the color of its imagery, I deem it worthy of being recalled. And then, who knows? If you, dear reader, happen to be a Benedictine friar distracted from spiritual pursuits by a pair of shining black eyes; if instead of concentrating on your prayers you are assaulted by the thought of a beautiful neck, or a splendid back, or some other briefly glimpsed rotundity at odds with the austerity of your calling, then you may be well advised to do as he says: "Think that a crack opens in the ground, through which you can see the flames of hell; that the smoke lifts up in currents that bring to your nose the sulphurous stench; that you lie in your deathbed breathing stertorously your last whiffs, in which you perceive the rotting emanations of all your limbs; that you see the souls of the damned as one sees them in paintings, writhing amid tongues of flame, surrounded by snakes, toads, and ugly lizards, whose rabid and furious bites enhance their pain, and whom they desperately bite in their turn; that you find yourself in the presence of your Savior, Jesus Christ, who threatens you, flamigerous sword in hand; that you see him, sitting on the throne that he shall raise in the Valley of Iosaphath, in the attitude of fulminating, with a most terrible countenance, those guilty ones that have received the sentence from which there is no appeal. . . ." And so on.

Who, after parading these terrible scenes before his mind, will remain obstinate? What kind of lust is it that continues unchanged after being brutally exposed to this atrocious, anti-erotic climate? The illness would be too far gone, virtually terminal, that would not respond with some alteration after this violent shock therapy. Unfortunately, it is clear that in times less pious than those of our therapist, the impact of this theological fire and brimstone tends to lose its force. But perhaps the good father had the impious or the irreligious in mind when he suggested alternatives devoid of scriptural reference. He volunteered one imaginative device when he said that he was horrified almost beyond endurance by a scene of dismemberment that he had seen or heard about (whether one or the other is irrelevant, provided the mental image was vivid). Others may find death by fire or by other violent means the most horrible. But he, as a kind of illustrative personal idiosyncrasy, could not stand the thought of dismemberment. Hence, his most effective defense against the stealthy attacks of erotic love (was he ever in need of defending himself? He does not say) was the mental evocation of scenes of torture by dismemberment.

The problem with association of ideas is that we cannot always determine the manner in which they will associate. I could make my point clearer by citing the work of contemporary psychologists. I prefer, however, to quote a passage from Baudelaire.[5] The same point is made, and with considerably more beautiful style than psychologists are in the habit of displaying:

> I imagine your beloved ailing. Her beauty has disappeared under the hideous crust of smallpox, like greenery under the heavy ices of winter. Still shaken by the long anguishes and the alternatives of the disease, you contemplate with sadness the unerasable stigmata on the body of the dear convalescing one; suddenly, in your ears resounds a "dying" melody, performed by the delirious bow of Paganini, and this sympathetic air talks to you about yourself and seems to tell you all your inner poem of lost hopes. —Since then, the traces of smallpox will talk to you about your happiness and will forever sing before your moved soul the mysterious air of Paganini. They will henceforth be not only an object of sweet sympathy, but even of physical voluptuousness, if you chance to be one of those sensitive spirits for whom beauty is above all the *promise* of happiness. It is therefore the association of ideas that makes one love the ugly woman; for you risk heavily, if your pockmarked mistress betrays you, not to be able to console yourself with other than a pockmarked woman.

Imagine an enemy thriving under the blows delivered to him with intent of exterminating him. Imagine every thrust giving him strength, and every effort to crush him actually fortifying him. Of such a foe we would infer the nature demoniac and the threat invincible. For the devil alone is credited with such properties, malignant in such a way as to exactly reverse our expectations. Not in vain did medieval demonologists invoke the Evil One with spells that were prayers in reverse, and assumed his worship to be a mock ceremonial that inverted the prescribed order of the saintly liturgy. Such a demoniac reversal erotic love may enact; of such devilish inversion is erotic passion fully capable. Who would have warned the Benedictine of the risk inherent in his technique? Of two mental pictures, one is attractive, the other repellent. How could he have anticipated that by prolonging their mutual association the repugnant would become attractive and the pleasing would repel? This paradox takes place in the world of reality. Many begin by associating pleasure with pain, in order, perhaps, to make pleasure painful, and end up finding pain pleasurable. The world topsy-turvy: not the least of paradoxes issued from the erotic. Even as our candid friar sat down to pen his original remedy for love, drawing his examples from the good gospel, another man, in another country, was busy writing the evil gospel. Untiringly, obsessively, by the trembling light of a candle, in the bottom of some dank dungeon—as was fitting decor for his somber production—that man toiled without cease to complete the awesome inventory of all the possible permutations and combinations of erotic pleasure and pain. The man was the Marquis de Sade. But his life and exploits merit a separate chapter.

THE DIVINE MARQUIS

I must talk of murders, rapes and massacres,
Acts of black nights, abominable deeds,
Complots of mischief, treason, villanies,
Ruthful to hear, yet piteously perform'd.

(Shakespeare, *Titus Andronicus*
Act V, sc. i, 64–68)

My wife is neither prudish, nor anti-intellectual. Nevertheless, upon reading one of the works of the Marquis de Sade, she reacted in a way that has come to be regarded as typical of the complacent bourgeois mentality: She was deeply and genuinely offended. Without saying a word, and having gone through about one-third of the book, she flung the slim volume into the trashcan and went straight to the bookshelves to look for a substitute—the apposite word might be an *antidote*—for her interrupted reading.

Noticing that the cause of her displeasure was a novel of the infamous marquis, I timidly represented my surprise at the vehemence of her reaction. After all, Sade and his work have remained a constant and worldwide preoccupation among intellectuals for about two centuries. Moreover, his influence has extended far beyond the strictly literary world: Theologians have been enraged, and psychiatrists have been intrigued; and even political scientists have been tickled, for some have culled examples of the class struggle from the vivid descriptions of victimization that are owed to the poisonous pen of the marquis. But my spouse was not in the mood to discuss the possibility that her impulsive judgment might have been in error. Making light of the ever-accruing mass of commentary, exegesis, and reinterpretation (or of the fact that the respected *Encyclopaedia Britannica* devotes greater space to this reprobate than to many a great benefactor of humanity), she made it known that her assessment was final. Emulating the verdict passed by a United States judge who once avoided the subtleties that confound the definition of pornography, my wife pronounced: "I know smut when I see it."

In the interest of domestic harmony, no more arguments were bandied on that occasion. But I could not avoid admiring a novelist who so incensed his readers. For writing is, like all communication, dialogue. It is saying something to someone, so that a writing is successful in the measure that it tends a bridge between two human hearts; there is no canon that prescribes an obligatory pleasing nature to its message. The worst disparagement to a speaker is for us to sit politely through his entire peroration while our attention drifts here and there, and we announce by our vapid smile that the speech will be forgotten even before it reaches its end. But if he angers us and compels us to leave the room in trembling agitation and forgetting the simple rules of decorum, his power will have been acknowledged. It is the same with books. Through the open pages a speaker tries to reach us. We feel sometimes amused, sometimes instructed, often irritated, and all too often bored. But now and then, in the lively gestures of the invisible speaker who addresses us from the printed pages, there comes an electric jolt that either glues us, galvanized, to the pages, or forces us to cast them off in a reflex response to the sparks that scald our fingers. A writer, if sincere, would rather see his book thrown into the trashcan with this irate conviction than politely relegated, with gentle oblivion, to the shelves of infinite boredom.

Justine was the sample of our author that the trashcan had welcomed with a ringing metallic sound. Rather—and let this be said in extenuation of my wife's outburst—a poor translation of the most cruelly obscene version of *Justine*. For it should be noted that Sade wrote at least three known versions of this work: the second more than twice the length of the first one, and the third one—about 1400 pages!—three times the length of the second. Its theme, "the misfortunes of virtue," is well known. Its plot is really of little relevance: A sweet orphan girl, virtuous and innocent, is made the butt of every conceivable infamy and abuse in a series of episodes painted with brilliance and imagination. For instance, dismissed at fourteen years of age from the convent in which she had been educated, she must defend her virtue from the assaults of debauchees who offer financial ease in exchange for sexual favors. She stoutly defends her moral principles and sees herself lowered to the position of servant in the household of an avaricious man. This one tries to induce her to steal from a neighbor. She refuses, and in reprisal she is accused falsely of theft and imprisoned. By becoming an accomplice in an arson that kills several prisoners, she succeeds in escaping, only to be raped in the woods of Bondy. She takes refuge in the castle of the young Count of Bressac, who turns out to be another monster: homosexual, cruel, perverse, sodomite, and unfilial. Because she refuses to help him in poisoning his mother, she is nearly devoured by the count's ferocious mastiffs loosed against her. Picked up by another libertine, she is branded with a hot iron and expelled. She encounters a group of pilgrims on their way to visit the miraculous Virgin of Saint-Mary-in-the-Woods. She joins them and is led to an abbey. Wouldn't you know it? The abbots of the place turn out to be lubricious and murderous perverts who kidnap her and make her the toy of their sensual, criminal pleasures for six months. And so on. In the end, after a series of vicissitudes during which she suffers indignities, abuses, and violence of every description, the wretched Justine finds a safe haven. It would seem that she has earned the right to rest after her uninterrupted victimization. The reader expects a belated recompense for a life of steadfast allegiance to virtue in the face of mean and unflagging assaults of vice. No such thing. With depressing consistency, our novelist makes heaven the unforgiving persecutor of virtue. Justine, whose attachment to right conduct wavered not one inch in the midst of allurements, temptations, and tortures, is now going to be fulminated. She is fatally struck by lightning in the terrible summer storm of the thirteenth day of July, in the year of our Lord 1788.

What are we to make of this succession of tortures, whippings, flayings, incisions, burns, poisonings, vivisections, beatings, and humiliations? The least sophisticated reader promptly realizes that this literature cannot be read like any other literature. For one thing, the plot is wholly irrelevant. The exterior events are obviously unimportant. Moreover, they are impossible. Those crapulous personages multiply their ecstatic, orgasmic experiences beyond any semblance of reality, page after page, and we come to understand why the artists of surrealist affiliation claimed this nightmarish, hallucinating narrator as their precursor and prophet.

Centuries of literary tradition had accustomed us to consider the writer's art as "mirror to nature." The writer holds his mirror to an external reality, and this independent world, with the serried objects that compose it, reflects itself on the polished surface. The reader gazes into it and passes a judgment on the degree of concordance between his own perception of the world of reality and what he sees reflected on the mirror. Details may appear revealed with meridian clarity that were only a blur to the reader. If so, this one will feel that he has been instructed. Or the image will please precisely on account of the subdued hues and soft contours that it gathers, excluding all sharp angularities and tawdry colors: The reader will be soothed, comforted in the thought that there are other ways of looking at the world. And even when the image is found imperfect or distorted, the autonomy of real object and reflected image is not in question.

Sade, however, arrives on the stage of received opinion with an unreflecting contraption that we cannot call a mirror. It does not in the least look like a mirror. And we are ready to dismiss it as a useless gadget when, suddenly, the surface is teeming with images: truculent, grotesque, hurtful, arresting, and lively. Not the passive reflection of a given reality, autonomous from the observer, but the active emanations of a mind that, like a film projector, shoots them up on the screen for the contemplation of an amazed and horrified spectator. Each image is, therefore, already a digested concept, a second-order idea, a symbol. Justine is not an innocent girl who goes through life suffering an endless series of vexations and injuries. Who can believe in the plausibility of such a personage? Never did an innocent maiden suffer one-tenth of that abuse without 'learning' or modifying her behavior. Justine, therefore, is a symbol. She is a symbol of Sade's bold contention that all our noble impulses are a hoax, and cruelty the only abiding reality of the human condition. And if it be true that all in Sade is symbolic, then Jean Paulhan[1] is correct when he says that Justine goes her way hand in hand with Cinderella, "for when it is said that Cinderella wore crystal slippers, we do not understand (unless we be thick as a board) that she was shod in glass shoes, but that she placed her feet with infinite delicacy." And therefore Paulhan's paradoxical conclusion may be maintained without too great an effort, that Sade's work, a compendium of unimaginable brutalities and crimes, ought to be read in the same way as one reads fairy tales.

The allegory of "the misfortunes of virtue" is complemented by that of *The Prosperities of Vice*. A quick notation at the end of the *Justine* manuscript states: "Finished at the end of fifteen days, on July 8, 1784." And as soon as this work is completed, the author is attacking its continuation, *Juliette, or The Prosperities of Vice*. Juliette is Justine's sister. She, too, had to leave the convent at a tender age. But instead of struggling to preserve her innocence, she heartily embraces a life of dissipation. She becomes a poisoner at the service of a murderous politician and is rewarded with riches and luxury. She joins the Society of Friends of Crime and gains access to honors and worldly distinctions. She travels through Italy, prostituting herself everywhere, and everywhere being admitted in the richest courts, the most opulent palaces, not excluding the pope's mansion. Her life is a series of acts of profligacy and wanton sensuality, each one earning Juliette still higher honors, social esteem, and money. In one version of *Justine,* the unhappy but virtuous sister roams the forests in wretched destitution. She encounters a beautiful noblewoman in the company of richly attired gentlemen. The exalted lady is Juliette, who embraces her sister tenderly and hears the relation of her martyrdom. She replies by recounting her own life, starting with these words: "As for me, my child, I chose the road of vice. I encountered nothing but roses."

Who created this topsy-turvy system of ethics? The life of the Apostle of Evil is itself a novel. He was born in the noble mansion of Prince Louis Henri, on June 2, 1740. Baptized in the church of Saint-Sulpice, he received the triple name Donatien Alphonse François as befitted his exalted social station. For there was no dearth of noble titles awaiting him. Through the maternal line he descended from an ancient lineage of the nobility of Provence. His titles included: lord of La Coste and Saumane, *coseigneur* of Mazan, lieutenant general of the provinces of Bresse, Bugey, Valromey, and Gex, and field marshal of the royal cavalry. Of his early years little is known. On May 17, 1763, with the approval of the royal family, he married the daughter of a wealthy magistrate, a member of the *petite noblesse*, Renée-Pélagie de Montreuil. And four months after this marriage (he is twenty-three years old), we find him incarcerated in the prison of Vincennes. The charges: outrage to public morals, blasphemy, and profanation of the image of Christ. In spite of his influential position he cannot avoid spending two weeks in prison. For the next four years, he leads a dissolute life, keeping several courtesans, and at one time even contriving to "pass" one of these for his legally wedded wife. No major scandal, however: a life no more and no less irregular than that of a large number (perhaps the majority) of privileged men of his time. Then comes the famous *affaire* Keller.

On Easter Day, April 3, 1768, at 9:00 A.M., Sade finds himself at the place-des-Victoires, dressed in gray jacket, white ornamental cuffs protruding around his wrists, sporting a stylish cane, and carrying an elegant hunting knife at the waist. He stands under the shadow of a statue of Louis XIV (that was to be destroyed by an angry mob in 1792), and from this observation post he sights a young woman who seems to be a beggar. She is Rose Keller, a German immigrant, thirty-six years old, the widow of a baker, struggling to eke out a living in prerevolutionary Paris. She can spin cotton, thread flax, wash linen, flail grain, and do sundry menial tasks to survive, but in these harsh times she has been reduced to beggary. The young marquis (he is now twenty-eight years of age) approaches her with the promise of one *écu* if she agrees to follow him. She draws back, diffident, replying that she is an honest woman. Sade reassures her: He is in need of a domestic, someone to put order in his household and clean his bedroom. After some interchange, Rose Keller accepts the offer and climbs into the carriage that the marquis, with a sign of his hand, has just summoned. And the two are off to Arcueil, a neighboring town where the nobleman has a country residence, much frequented by those who cater to his bizarre sexual preferences. In fact, his valet, Langlois, has recently brought two girls who are still in the house this very moment, when the marquis arrives with the new visitor.

Although the two had barely exchanged a word during the nearly three-hour-long journey, trepidating over country roads, the woman is not surprised to be taken directly to his bedroom, upstairs, since this room was specifically mentioned in the transaction as the place where her services would be most needed. The marquis tells her that he is going to bring some refreshment to give her, and to wait for him in the bedroom. When he leaves, he locks the room with two turns of the key. He goes, instead, to prepare himself for the uncommon act that occupied his mind during the journey. Presumably, he pays a visit to the two girls his valet has earlier procured, for a kind of sexual warm-up. After a while, he appears in the bedroom and orders Rose to follow him. Although it is still afternoon, the shut wooden sashes of the barred windows and the thick stone walls of the country residence render the place as dark and silent as if it were late at night. This is why the marquis is holding a lighted candle in his left hand. But there is more elaborate detail to be remarked in the attire of this ritual-conscious young man. Instead of the gray jacket that he wore at the place-des-Victoires this morning, he now dons a sleeveless garment; his naked arms emerge unencumbered, free from the dressy, laced manches that covered them before. A colorful detail should be remarked in our man: Not neglecting the functional details, he has also tied a handkerchief around his forehead.

According to Keller's declaration to the police, this is how it all happened. Once in the appropriate room, he summarily orders her to take off her clothes. She is reticent. She asks why. He says it is "to have fun." She retorts, indignant, that she did not come for that. Then, tired of this annoying preamble, Sade draws his knife (same hunting knife that he was carrying in the morning) and threatens: Either she does as she is told, or she is a dead woman. Trembling, Keller yields to this persuasion. The marquis, with renewed threats to his victim, succeeds in tying her limbs to the wooden posts of a canopied bed. The scenario is thus complete: There is a psychopath who has contrived to attire himself in colorful executioner's garb; a piteously frightened, naked, bound female victim lying in ventral decubitus; and a dark, silent torture chamber, barely illuminated by the trembling light of a candle. The torture itself is less awesome than these ceremonial surroundings. The torturer discharges vigorous blows on the victim's posterior bodily eminences by means of a leather whip on which knots have been tied, expressly for the purpose. The

ON THE NATURE OF THINGS EROTIC

victim wails and shrieks, and the torturer silences her with threats of his dagger. Clearly, the man is working himself up to a climax, because his blows become nervously reiterative, until at last, "swearing and uttering most fearful screams," he stops, seemingly in coincidence with his orgasmic release. The torture is over.

After this harrowing scene, the torturer shows some kindness. He daubs some ointment on the excoriated skin, unties the weeping victim, and gives the woman instructions to rinse the bloodstains off her clothes in a water basin nearby. He gives her some bread, and wine, and some broth, and tells her to rest for a while. He then leaves the room, locking the door behind him. Rose Keller loses no time. She manages to pry the window open, and using the bedsheets and some of her clothes tied into a makeshift rope, she squeezes herself through the barred window and lowers herself to the ground below. She is in Fontaine Street in the village of Arcueil. Langlois, the marquis's valet, runs after her, asking her to come back and saying that his master wishes to speak to her. But she will have no more to do with the bizarre employer. Langlois pulls out a bag with money, offering to pay her generously for her services. But she does not stop running.

Rose Keller comes across some village women. They are startled at her unkempt, disheveled condition, and her bloody dress. Tearfully, Rose explains her distress and describes her recent ordeal. Among exclamations of astonishment and disbelief, she is taken to the shed of a farmhouse, where the women lift up her skirts to see for themselves. That man is a monster! A demon! Indignant and shocked, the women take the trembling victim to the authorities for a deposition. After the case is vented in criminal court, an order of arrest is issued. In June

1768, our man is behind bars in the prison of Pierre-Encise. He will remain there for close to a year.

Much has been written about this episode in the life of Donatien Alphonse François. The details of the events were recorded in the depositions of witnesses, lawyers, and law enforcement agents, but as with all events centered around human actions, a straightforward interpretation is impossible. Was Rose Keller an innocent victim, or did she, driven by hunger, come to the house fully disposed to satisfy Sade's sexual demands, only to discover that her customer's licker-ishness was of a type that could easily get out of hand? The ease of her evasion and the discrepancies between her own report of the violence suffered and the lesions described by the examining physician have been said to suggest that some exaggeration was deliberately introduced in the plaintiff's filed grievance. It now appears likely that circumstances extraneous to the described facts had a bearing on the severe sentence that was passed against the offender. The truth is, a powerful and influential nobleman of Sade's rank *could* and often *did* get away with murder in those times. When high-ranking aris-tocrats were involved as suspects, incidents of this kind were often hushed by venal authorities. But this time much was made of the sociopolitical context (a powerful aristocrat wan-tonly abusing a member of the lower classes), and even of the religious undertones of the misdeed (the lashing, in Holy Week, could have been a sacrilegious mockery of the passion of Christ). Public opinion was conspicuously whipped up against the ar-bitrariness of an individual aristocrat, by a government that merrily went its irresponsible way until the very moment of universal collapse. Historians conclude, from evidence that for the sake of brevity we omit, that powerful parties had decided to "contain" Sade's misconduct, and members of his own family had agreed on the prudence of such counsel.

Be that as it may, the stray sheep is strictly confined, in the merciless manner that was customary at the time. He is thrown into a dank dungeon that may well have inspired Piranesi, and permission for the prisoner to take fresh air in daily walks outside his cell is not granted until after one month has passed. Red tape, parsimonious by nature, seemed to be much more so when impelled by the ponderous and malfunctioning wheels of the *ancien régime,* itself in terminal condition. Permission for his wife to visit him comes only after the fifth month of his internment.

We hear very little from the "divine" marquis until 1772, the year of the famous *affaire* of Marseille. Of this incident the documentation is massive. All biographers of Sade contribute great profusion of details, for, to a greater extent than in the former scandal, official acts and depositions of witnesses accrued in the legal suits undertaken against him by several plaintiffs.

In mid-June he leaves his homestead in Provence to obtain some cash in Marseille. He is in his early thirties. It would not be reasonable to expect that a man of his age, life-style, proclivities, and money would have passed the opportunity to make the most out of his stay in the city. Accordingly, his servant, Latour, has preceded him, charged with the duty of scouring the streets and houses of ill fame in search of the appropriate feminine bodies. His master's instructions have been as clear as they were specific: He wants them "very young."

So it is that in the morning of June 27, Sade and his servant enter the domicile of Mariette Borélly, a twenty-three-year-old madam, at the corner of Aubagne and Capucins streets. Three girls, between eighteen and twenty years of age, are already waiting for the customers. The specific nature and arrangement of the scenes of sexual activity, and even the chronological order in which they took place, are a matter of historical record. One biographer,[2] with that irrepressible penchant for order that the French make a point of national pride, has actually systematized the scenes of the orgy into six: five with three simultaneous participants, and one in which only Sade and one of the girls, Marianne, shared the spotlight. I will dispense with this Gallic attention to detail and love of system. Suffice it to say that in the course of these proceedings great inventiveness was displayed. The variety that Sade pursued—subject, of course, to the obligatory finiteness of possible combinations—was astonishing. With this limitation, Sade disported himself as his usual enthusiastic stage manager: He directed the twosomes and threesomes into striking scenes of sodomization, homosexuality, mutual flagellation, and, to break the monotony, as it were, normal heterosexual activity.

In the intervals of these exhausting exertions, the marquis displayed all the gallantry and all the delicacy of manners that a man of his high station, bred in the ways of the most refined court in the world, could, on the occasion, manifest. Thus, he joked with the girls, rewarded their submissiveness with liberality, and tried to win their unreserved acceptance. His bringing with him a crystal box of exquisite workmanship filled with chocolates, which he offered insistently to the girls, was seen as part of his effort to ingratiate himself with the merry company. Marianne, but not the other girls, partook abundantly of the offered sweets.

The chocolate box was only half full when that same evening Sade carried it with him to the street of Saint-Férréol-le-Vieux on his way to visit Marguerite Coste, another woman of ill fame. Even after the morning excesses, a young and still vigorous libertine could evidently itch with renewed fancies as soon as things started to become a little boring in the evening. Thus, Sade engages once again in one of his favorite stage games, with Madame Coste this time, although, it must be said, the staged composition consists this time of a single act: the flesh is weak. Much to her misfortune, Marguerite Coste has a sweet tooth. When Sade leaves her house, the crystal chocolate box is totally empty.

In the official investigation that followed it was established that Marguerite Coste had suddenly been taken by violent abdominal pains, a feeling of urinary urgency, and protracted vomiting of blackish, grumous stomach contents. The next day, a pale, weak Marianne was brought to the police headquarters, leaning on the shoulders of two friends, and in the company of several other girls of Aubagne Street. Together with seven other witnesses, she set down in her deposition that an attempt at poisoning was traceable to the chocolates that "a foreigner" had liberally distributed among various women. Marianne is not quite recovered from the intoxication. She suffered prostration, vomiting of sanguineous secretions, and passing of bloody urine.

The legal machinery is once again activated against the infamous marquis, but this one, forewarned that the state means business, flees from his castle of La Coste toward Italy. The crown continues the legal proceedings in his absence. The two felons, Sade and Latour, are declared *contumax et défaillants,* contumacious and in contempt of court. The sentence is passed on September 3. Sade and his servant, guilty of sodomy (a serious offense in the eighteenth century), poisoning attempts, and outrage to the country's morals, are condemned to do an act of public atonement, *amende honorable,* in front of the door of the cathedral, then to be transported to the gallows, "where the said sieur Sade shall have his head severed, and the said Latour shall hang from the gibbet and be strangled; thereafter the bodies of the said sieur Sade and the said Latour shall be cremated, and their ashes scattered in the wind." On September 12, after the Parliament of Provence has confirmed the sentence of the judges in Marseille, Sade and Latour, who cannot be found, are burned in effigy in the central plaza of the town of Aix. The two gallows birds are not in France. Latour accompanies his master in his tour of sunny Italy. Sade travels in high style, graciously accepting the honors due to his high position in the social scale. He is also accompanied by his sister-in-law, Mademoiselle de Launay, whom Sade has seduced, and who passes for his wife in the elegant circles of Italy.

On these highlights of the life of Sade all historians agree. But it is also established that the "monster" had no intention to kill. Behaving like the utterly irresponsible aristocrat that he was, he simply added childish touches to his grown-up misdeeds. The "poison" in the chocolates was a mixture of aniseed and cantharides. Aniseed is, as is well known, an aromatic seed. It has a carminative effect that, in the mind of the marquis, added unexpected delights to his uncommon practices. Cantharides are soft-bodied beetles of the genus *Cantharis,* popularly known as "Spanish flies" or "Russian flies," depending on the prevailing local prejudice. The technical name, *Cantharis vesicatoria,* alludes to the vesicant effect of ground preparations of these insects applied to the skin, due to the organic compound, *cantharidin* (of currently known chemical structure; unknown, of course, in Sade's time). This compound is eliminated by the urinary system when preparations of cantharides are ingested, and the irritation produced in the urethra has been accompanied by penile erection in men.

Observation of this phenomenon gave rise to the myth that cantharides' intake has an aphrodisiac effect. Not too long ago, one could still see cases of cantharides intoxication in North America: The victims were usually the unsuspecting love objects of desperate (but ill-informed) lovers who had fed them a cantharides overdose. This uncommon cause of poisoning is all but vanished, at least in industrialized countries with strict regulation of what may reach the public over the pharmacist's counter. But in Sade's time the product was easily available and its use widespread. During the Regency, "Richelieu's sweets" were dainties laced with cantharides powder, from which one may assume that the famous cardinal was not above the use of questionable strategies in his erotic undertakings, just as he seems not to have disdained trickery and deceit in matters ministerial.

It is a rare thing to see the life of a writer becoming one with his work; often the two run divergent courses. But in the orgy of Marseille, the marquis and his work are indistinguishable from each other. For Roland Barthes has written, in a brilliant essay on Sade,[3] that the marquis deals with the erotic as a grammarian, for whom the scenes of lasciviousness are formed by the same mental mechanism that leads to writing: Each new concupiscence is a unit (Barthes says "a pornogram") relating to the preceding and following ones as the units of discourse relate to each other. It seems true that in Sade vice is subordinated to words. In Marseille, he fully enacts his role as rhetorician of the erotic. Placing himself in the center of the room, he arranges, disposes, organizes, and commands every posture, every movement of the actors. He must, above all, name each new perversion; whether it be actually committed seems to us a secondary and unimportant fact. Somehow, the important thing is that the act be named.

In some of his productions it is easy to see Sade's vocation to be the "town crier" of vice, or the official denotator of debauch. His boldest work was not published until an erudite doctor, Eugene Duehren, brought it to public light in 1904. It is *120 Days in Sodom, or The School of Libertinage* ([Paris: Club des Bibliophiles, 1904], 543 pages, with a facsimile of one page of the original manuscript), written during a period of Sade's imprisonment in the Bastille. The manuscript was taken away from the author by his jailers, who gave it to a nobleman. It remained in the possession of the latter's family for three generations, until its publication in the present century. The plan of the novel, if it may be so called, is simple. Four enormously rich, strange personages, the Duke of Blangis, his brother, and two other men, conceive the extraordinary plan of tasting all the sexual perversions that were ever fancied by a deranged human imagination. The libertines engage the services of four old hags, former prostitutes turned procurers, whose duty it is to expose in a systematic narrative all the depravities of which they are aware, and which are no small number. For instance, the first one must describe 150 "simple" perversions; the second one, "rare and complicated aberrations," such as those requiring multiple participants; the third one, those perversions that lead to bodily tortures and might end in murder; the fourth one, the violence itself. Note the prominent place that is conceded to narrative, or denotation: The hideous women's chief duty is merely to describe. Vast sums of money are spent in acquiring young boys and girls for the planned orgy. On October 29, at 8:00 P.M., the proceedings start as the participants enter the duke's castle.

The daily routines are minutely described. The debauchees get up at 10:00 A.M. and visit the boys. They take a refreshment at 11:00 A.M., which consists of chocolate, roast beef, and some wine (kneeling nude girls serve them). They eat again from 3:00 P.M. until 5:00 P.M. They enter the recitation hall at 6:00. The recitation hall is semicircular. It has four great niches ornamented with mirrors, and an ottoman in a corner. Once again, description, oral narrative, reigns supreme: There is a throne in the center of the room for the beldam narrators, who take turns while discoursing on sexual perversion. The throne is covered with blue-black satin ornamented with cloth-of-gold. On the steps leading to the throne sit the enslaved "objects of debauch," whose duty it is to relieve the libertines, on demand, when these are set afire by the descriptions of the narrators. Various chambers adjoin the recitation hall, where at the end of the four-hour-long narrative the libertines put into practice what they have heard from the narrator. The sessions end at 2:00 in the morning.

The original manuscript of this work was written in thirty-seven days, inside a cell of the Bastille, in working sessions between the hours of 7:00 and 10:00 in the evening, and under conditions of extreme duress. Paper was not easily available to the prison's inmate-author. He wrote in tiny, compressed script, and on both sides of the page. Each sheet of paper measures eleven centimeters in greatest dimension. The sheets were joined end to end, lengthwise, so that the completed manuscript forms a long band that extends for twelve meters and ten centimeters. The last owner of this manuscript had rolled this paper band and placed it inside a cylindrical wooden box shaped like a phallus.

In surveying some of Sade's works, hardly a reader will not recoil, either in astonishment or in horror, at the frenzied imagination of this recluse. He conceives "a man who had procreated three children with his own mother, one of which was a girl whom he had given in marriage to his son. So that having intercourse with that girl, he actually had carnal commerce with his sister, daughter, and sister-in-law, and had forced his son to lie with his sister and mother-in-law." And he presents us with another incestuous father who is taken with the idea of using a sacred wafer in sexual practices with his married daughter, "so as to combine incest, adultery, sodomy, and sacrilegiousness." Yet it should not be forgotten that Sade is the taxonomist, compiler, and curator of vice, not the experimentalist. His terrifying *120 Days in Sodom,* perhaps the most devastating book of its genre ever conceived by human mind, is, undoubtedly, literature. Whatever else it might be (a clinical document for psychiatrists' researches, for instance), it is fundamentally a piece of writing, and at times one of an exalted kind; critics have remarked that the introduction is a masterpiece of French prose. The prison inmate saw no other way to vent his frustrations and to revenge himself from the society that deprived him of his freedom than to compose thick folios in a corner of his dungeon, therein to scowl at the world from misanthropic seclusion.

After the *affaire* of the poisoned sweets, Sade, returned to his country, is again thrown in jail. His life is spared through the intercession of friends. But what at first was merely an effort to contain him, at times instigated by relatives weary of the scandals that sullied the family's honor, soon becomes the harsh, merciless repression by a society that senses a threat to its integrity in the freedom of this man. Ten years in the Bastille, a month in the Conciergerie, two years in another fortress, fourteen years in Charenton, three years in Bicêtre, and one year in Saint-Pelagie: every new society constituted in France during the time of its most radical transformations found good reasons to lock him up. First the Old Regime, then the Republic, then the Terror, then the Consulate, and finally the Empire: For nearly thirty years of his life, the soul of this man roamed free, wild and unrestrained, furiously attacking all conventions, while his body languished in forced immobility, becoming stiff, lazy, and—a fact of which he bitterly complained toward the end of his life—ponderously fat. He might have believed for a moment, when the furious pickaxes of the revolutionists were cracking the hinges of his dungeon's door, that he was being freed by a triumphant phalanx of brother iconoclasts. The illusion did not last long. As soon as his new book comes off the press, the local militia drags him in front of a revolutionary tribunal, where an improvised judge reads to him out of the new constitution a section that says: "Corruptors of public morals are the enemies of the people." And there he is, back on bread and water. Not long thereafter, in the storm that agitates Europe, a flash of lightning rends the sky: Bonaparte. The Great Corsican's legions are razing the old monarchies and spreading the light of freedom; a new dawn shines. In a fit of enthusiasm for the new order, Sade sends to the emperor an autographed copy of his most recent work. New disappointment. Outraged at the boldness of the descriptions, the undisguised sexual frenzies, and the disregard of all moral precepts, the emperor orders Sade's internment in an asylum for the insane. With this aggravating turn: Bonaparte wishes to see to it personally that all freedom of mobility and expression be denied to this dangerous man.

The man is, indeed, dangerous. Were he unlucky enough to have survived to our day, I sincerely doubt that he would walk the streets. We have not learned yet to look calmly at what he used to relish; we would find, no doubt, valid reasons to take him behind bars. And I do not mean his sexual deviancy. In this regard it would be fair to claim that we have grown tolerant and, with some reservations, more enlightened.

Sexual sadism and its inevitable corollary, masochism, continue to be mysterious, puzzling paradoxes (consider the puzzle: Pleasure is shunned, pain is looked for; but if pain pleases, it is no longer pain, but pleasure; yet it pleases because it pains; but pain, by definition, excludes pleasure . . . etc., etc. Or else: The masochist enjoys domination, but he orders the form of his abjection; he wishes to become an object but turns his tormentors into tools for his pleasure; he commands his own vassalage; but if he orders, he is not a vassal . . .), but we are close to believing that, as long as no coercion is exerted, people are free to indulge in whatever paradoxical behavior they choose. And why not? Sadism is but one among millions of contradictions that we risk by being alive.

In our day, the dangerousness of this man would not hinge on the logical strength of his system, but in the eighteenth century it may have been so. That was, we like to think, the Age of Reason. And Sade's pestilential pages come prepackaged in a reasoning format that must have been pure dynamite in those days. When Bressac tries to persuade Justine to assist him in poisoning his mother, truly noble paragraphs of eighteenth-century prose are arrayed in support of his argumentation: The power to destroy a fellow human being is illusory; man has no power to destroy; at most he changes the forms of nature. All forms weigh the same in the eyes of nature, where nothing is created or destroyed, but merely transmuted. "What does ever-changing nature care that this mass of flesh, today conforming a woman, be reproduced tomorrow under the guise of a thousand different insects?" That the misdeed is about to be perpetrated on his own mother hardly troubles Bressac, heartless and unshakable to the end, like all Sadeian villains. "What! Would I be stopped by this vain consideration? Why should I? Was this mother thinking of me when in her lustful abandon she conceived the fetus out of which I developed? Am I obligated to be grateful to her for having thought of her own pleasure?" And this frightful unfilial tirade is buttressed by arguments derived from biology (today obsolete and false) demonstrating that the male seed only contributes to the formation of the fetus. To Sade's credit, the objections raised by Justine depicting the torments that remorse brings after a crime are no less vivid and as eloquent as the exhortation to the poisoning. Bressac, annoyed by Justine's attitude but unmoved by her plea, postpones the execution of his crime. Many are the occasions in which Justine is forced to invoke the terrible pains of remorse to dissuade evildoers. But her appeals clash against the baseness of Sadeian "heroes," whose attitude is voiced in this terrible reply: "Don't you see, Justine? Man does not repent of what he is in the habit of doing. Get used to evil, and remorse will vanish. If you so much as feel a twinge of remorse after having committed a crime, commit still another one. Ten, twenty, or thirty evil actions shall remove all possibility of remorse. The proof is in the many living examples of what people call 'hardened criminals.' " One of Sade's bloodcurdling personages summarizes this chilling philosophy, which retains today all its unsettling tone: "Just as stupidity leads people to faith, so does crime render them impassive. There you have the best proof that virtue is to man but a superficial principle."

For statements of this kind, if too insistently and successfully reiterated—*Justine* sold six editions in the first two years of its issuance—Sade today, I am afraid, would not remain a free man indefinitely.

Suppose we could bring back some of Sade's contemporaries. Rousseau the novelist would still thrill us if he could work among us, provided he made some concessions to modern usage. But I truly doubt that anyone would take him seriously as the political scientist, sociologist, and philosopher that he fancied he was. Diderot, "the father of witty conversation," might make it big in the lecture circuit, but academicians would spurn him for losing time in trifles. Dr. Johnson would have some following, but I am afraid he would not reach a mass audience. Television would be out of the question for the good doctor. Why, with all that winking, lip-smacking, snorting, and shoulder-shrugging (medical historians have suggested that a neurological disorder made him gesture grotesquely), he would never be as successful as our well-groomed TV speakers. Voltaire, of course, could do anything. He would thrill us, and instruct us, and amuse us. The problem is, over-preoccupied with the Church, he would continue thundering about irrationality in Christian doctrine, and critics would ask why such a genius insists in wasting his talents on topics that are no longer "relevant."

Sade alone would terrify. For Sade alone would stand apart from all these great men, and in the isolation of his cell (for, surely, we would imprison him) would continue distilling the nihilistic tenets of a philosophy whose central tenet simply says *Le prochain ne m'est rien* (the brotherhood of man means nothing to me). Let others repeat the fallacious and hypocritical commonplaces; let them say that the relation between men must be subordinated to a higher value surpassing the singular individualities, and bestowing upon all a sort of collective transcendence. Lies! "Man is alone in the world. All creatures are born in isolation, and without any need for each other." The only possible relationship that Sade admits is that of crime, or of carnal concupiscence. For these passions, he says, link human beings by virtue of having two senses: "one very unfair with respect to the victim; the other one eminently fair with respect to the one who exerts it."

Two centuries after Sade, we have continued to repeat to ourselves that a larger plan integrates all men into the universal community and rules, or ought to rule, their behavior. This proposition is variously formulated: All men are brothers, inasmuch as they are children of God. Or, all men intuitively recognize their fraternity. Or, all men are conscious of a transcendent link that joins them to their brethren. Simultaneous with the framing of these statements, we have behaved as if such a link did not really exist. We have stood indifferent to genocide in Germany, while it occurred; and to mass extermination of similar scale in Vietnam, Cambodia, and Laos, to name only a few recent hecatombs. It is worthy of note that while the carnage was going on, we felt, in all candor, quite at ease. The record will show that the entire world looked upon with glee or utter indifference at horrifying past deeds, and that millions in Vancouver, Beijing, or Australia lose no sleep over thousands upon thousands of unfair killings in Central America. Everyone knows it. For, tell me, how could one live if one were deeply troubled by these things? ("Don't you see, Justine? Men are not disturbed for doing what they do by habit.") In other words, millions of men die unjustly, at the hands of other men, *all the time*. And our response to this is: "I know it, and that is quite sufficient. Enough said; spare me the gory details." But suppose someone were rash enough to persist. Assume a man were to be found who kept describing, denoting, copying, with lifelong, obsessive insistence, all the details and horrors of all crimes. Woe to him! An entire society, bristling with indignation, would crush this hideous violator of its accepted standards. Who knows, if the pestilent descriptions were to fall into unprepared hands . . . Why, the young might be induced to raping, or thieving, or killing! Worded differently, all the outrage that slumbered during the actual performance of wholesale atrocity is suddenly awake and ready to punish the man who, by being too spirited and imaginative a portraitist, *might* misguide the incautious. Would we not punish such a man, just as his countrymen did? It would feel so good to punish a single rape after having stood indifferent face to the sacrifice of millions!

Sade, of course, went too far. Not only did he dare to shake the complacency of society, but he also made of it a profession of faith. Not only was he the denotator of crime in its infinite morphologies, but he also built a system with his denotations. He dared to maintain that the fundamental relationship between human beings is not one subordinate to a higher, supra-individual value, but purely and simply this one: violence and cruelty. "The merit of Sade," wrote Simone de Beauvoir,[4] "is not only to have cried loudly what all confess shamefully to themselves: it is to have taken sides. Instead of indifference, he chose cruelty. And this is why he finds so many echoes today, when the individual is aware of being the victim not so much of the malice of men, as of their good conscience."

SOME VIEWS ON WOMEN, PAST AND PRESENT

The Past

To watch the rashness with which men and women have always abandoned themselves to the impulse that draws them together, one would never have guessed that they did so with serious misgivings. It would seem, on the surface, that the natural impetus was left unquestioned. For to cavil at laws natural and inflexible, like fretting because there is ebb and flow in tides or because nights succeed days in regular alternation, seems unpardonable folly. And yet it is well known that men not always agreed, in their hearts, with the natural order of things. The need to seek women often seemed to them a vexation; and the sentiments annexed to man-woman pairing since time immemorial, irreconcilable with their view of the world. It is well known that the ancient Greek philosophers seriously debated the merits of a popular alternative, homosexual love. The debate remains the subject of unending scholarly research. A review of this material would fill the space of no small a library. In the present essay, it will be necessary to allude to only few of the treatments of the problem in classical antiquity.

Early in the fourth century A.D., Lucian (or one of his imitators) wrote his *Dialogue on Two Types of Love*.[1] In it, Charicles argues for the supremacy of man-woman erotic relationships, whereas Callicratides defends the view that male homosexuality is more praiseworthy. Charicles's speech opens up with the argument that we may term of "naturalness." Life would be uncorrupted if all men adhered to the plan of nature, taken as the design of Providence. The rhetoric gains momentum with allusions to the universal character of heterosexuality in the natural world: wolves mate with she-wolves, boars seek to lie with sows, and tigers lie with tigresses. In due season, all male animals are infused with desire for the females of their kind. Neither birds soaring on high, nor moles under the ground, nor fish and other creatures whose whole lifespan courses entirely underwater, says Charicles, are ever seen struggling to achieve sexual intercourse with fellow males. And what is more, ancient times never witnessed such bizarre event among males of the human species. A perversion of instincts, therefore, is the only explanation that can account for this strange inclination that leads some men "to pursue what they ought to avoid, and to avoid what they ought to pursue." And having thus shown that this inclination is contrary to the plan of nature, the speaker warns us of the obvious, namely that it is inimical to the preservation of the race. For, clearly, if all were to fall into this depravity, mankind would cease to exist.

Leaving the argument of "naturalness," Charicles turns to what may be called the argument of "utilitarianism." He proposes to show that the enjoyment derived from women is, to men, far superior to that provided by men. First, because it is longer lasting, and second, because it is better shared. The beauty of woman, we are reminded, lasts longer than that of man. In the colorful expression that Lucian places in Charicles's mouth, woman remains from maidenhood to middle age "a pleasant armful for a man to embrace." And this juncture provides him with the opportunity to embark on a panegyric of woman's beauty, and how it undergoes transformations without suffering detriment along the successive stages of her reproductive life. Nubile freshness is no doubt attractive, but the seductive grace of a ripe, experienced matron is no less charming. It is otherwise with boys. Man's limbs are delicate only until puberty; thenceforward they grow stout and hard. The rounded features of the boy become angular in the man; the smooth, soft skin of that one turns into the rough, bristle-covered epidermis of this one. In the very special idiosyncrasy of ancient Greek males, the erotic value of men was extremely short-lived. The sophist Bion used to call the sprouting beards of pubescent lovers "Aristogeiton," in allusion to an Athenian tyrannicide. Because, explained this wit of illustrious Greece, as the hair grew it had the effect of freeing the older lover from a beautiful tyranny. Durable liaisons of two males (as in our day, I might add) were quite rare; the few known were often quoted as shining examples of steadfast affection. As to the argument that we might call of "egalitarianism," I prefer to skip its details. By somewhat crass reference to the physical operations of lovemaking, Charicles concludes that pleasure is shared more evenly between partners of different sex than between those belonging to the same sex.

Lastly, Charicles develops the argument of "reductionism": If we are ready to approve of homosexuality among men, we might as well let women make love to each other, too. And here we are somewhat surprised to see how this defender of heterosexuality, who has just made an eloquent speech on woman's beauty, now damns her defendant with faint praise. He first draws a negative picture of lesbianism and then admonishes men on the impropriety of imitating such disgusting example. Reductionism blends into male supremacism. How much better that a woman should fall into those repugnant excesses than that the nobility of the male sex should be degraded by becoming effeminate and assuming the part played by the "lower" sex! With this impassioned epilogue, the speech comes to a defiant close.

Callicratides now comes forward to defend the opposite view. In the very fact that homosexuality is regarded as "unnatural" by his opponent, Callicratides is going to ground the supremacy of erotic love between males. It is not an aberration, he contends. It is a refinement, an improvement. Love of women is nature's expedient to secure the perpetuation of the race, but love of men "is a noble duty enjoined by a philosophic spirit." Whereas in the eyes of Charicles it has seemed abhorrent because unenforced by nature, in the eyes of Callicratides it seems noble because unnecessary. It is not enjoined by inflexible necessity; rather, it is cultivated by those who judge it beautiful. The grounds for its promotion are aesthetic. And beauty is in all superior to necessity. Human existence rose from an inferior to a superior status. As long as human life was a beastly struggle against a harsh environment, men remained ignorant of the supreme forms of pleasure. As men advanced on the road of progress, their mores adapted to their progressively more exalted condition.

Callicratides skillfully links the prevalence of homosexuality with the blossoming of arts and crafts (in ancient Greece, I suppose, the argument was well taken). Intercourse with women was necessary in the early stages of human development so that mankind would not perish. But having ensured their survival, men began to strive for higher things. Just as no one would rightly maintain that feeding on wild roots and covering oneself with the coarse skins of wild animals is preferable to the delights and advantages of a refined cuisine and a modern clothing industry, so no one can say that heterosexuality is laudable on account of being old, or homosexuality blamable because it is of more recent onset. Indeed, old things may be necessary, but the new things that are added are often superior, since innovation is the fruit of leisure and the product of men of talent who, once freed from harsh toil, could apply their genius to invention. By the same token, lions, bears, boars, and tigers manifest urge only for the female of their species, but this is not surprising, since they are incapable of thought. "Lions do not have such love, because they are not philosophers, either. Bears have no such love, because they are ignorant of the beauty that comes from friendship."

To Charicles's rapturous exposition of the beauty of women, Callicratides now opposes an equally eloquent, misogynist speech. Women are vain. Their time is consumed amid ewers, basins, mirrors, jewels, dresses, and cosmetics. They are disloyal, untrustworthy. A man is a fool who would place his peace of mind in their hands. Whatever beauty they have is done away with through their abuse of cosmetics. "It is a shock to see them rise in the morning from last night's bed." They squander the husband's or lover's fortune. They are vacuous. They pass the day in gossip. Of what? "Of their heterosexual slumbers, and their beds fraught with femininity, on rising from which every man immediately needs a bath." In contrast, Callicratides invites us to survey the daily routines of a Greek boy, a model of orderly living. He rises at dawn and immediately washes with pure water—no need for him to cleanse red stains of rouge around the cheeks or the smudged black pigment around the eyes. He dresses in the *chiton,* a boy's undergarment, above which he places the *klamys,* or mantle for boys, and he is off to school and to the gymnasium. There, freshly anointed, he exercises and later practices on the writing tablets and listens to the philosophers. All the while, the gymnasiarchs see to it that nothing improper be done. Next, he learns to play the lyre. Then comes the wrestling school, which will prepare him to serve his country in the battlefield. Or he may go to training in horsemanship, where he will further strengthen his body while he learns to ride Thessalian horses. The day closes for this admirable and beautiful boy who, having thus "divided his time between wisdom, justice, temperance, and the strengthening of his body," is ready for a well-earned sleep. And after painting these contrasting scenes between male and female, the expositor ends with as lyrical a rhapsodizing as that of his predecessor. Who would deny that a being of this mental and bodily perfection and disciplined life is worthier of love and friendship than the great mass of women of his time?

Wherever the wits of classical antiquity gather together, we hear the same arguments bandied around. Plato's *Symposium, Phaedrus,* and *Lysis;* Xenophon's *Symposium;* and other important works all raise the question anew: whether man or woman is the proper object of man's affection. Not uncommonly, the judgment goes against woman.

In Plutarch's *Dialogue on Love*[2] Daphnaeus undertakes the defense of the union of man and wife, "than which there has not existed, now or ever, a fellowship more sacred." His interlocutor in the dialogue, Protogenes, remains unconvinced.

There is no harm in legislators singing the praises of hetero-sexuality, he says, since it is necessary for producing children. "But genuine Love has no connection with the women's quar-ters. I deny that it is love that you have felt for women and girls—any more than flies feel love for milk, or bees for honey, or than caterers and cooks for the calves and fowl they fatten in the dark." For an important sector of the Greek intelli-gentsia, the matter seemed quite settled: Lust for women is a necessary and normal appetite, but it is a mistake to say that it is love. Love can only be the proper fruit of friendship and virtue, and so defined it can only be the love of boys. The other kind, that which "spends its time in the bosoms and beds of women," is but a base and bastard sentiment, left to effeminates and incompatible with a generous and manly char-acter. It is of some interest to recollect that homosexuality was praised as manly, and heterosexuality disparaged as effeminate in ancient Greece. Courage is a virtue that shines brightest among true men, who feel love for boys, and not among those effeminate, soft and spoiled characters inclined to dalliances with unguent-drenched, face-painted women. At several points in the work of Plato, and repeated severally by other philos-ophers, the notion is expounded that the best army would be one constituted entirely by male homosexuals. For if a man and his boy-lover were deputized to face the enemy on the battlefield, neither one nor the other would suffer the shame of being seen in the grip of fear or revealed as cowardly in the eyes of his beloved. Pammenes, a politician, censured Homer for having arrayed the companies of Acheans by tribes and clans (*Iliad* II, 362), instead of stationing lover beside beloved. An army so constituted would never see shameful turntails and would never know defeat. In the words of an apologist of such a military regiment of "gay regulars": "It is a fact that men desert their fellow tribesmen and relatives and even (God knows) their parents and children; but lover and beloved, when their god [Eros] is present, no enemy has ever encountered and forced his way through."

It is useless to extend the description of the ancient debate. Feminist researches have often used it to show that the ancient world oppressed women with pitiless harshness, relegating them to the status of tools for reproduction, but denying them the humane feelings of friendship and affection that males reserved for other males only. To hear the tone of some speakers in the Greek dialogues and in some Roman works, one is compelled to admit that the accusation holds true for many prominent men in the ancient Greco-Roman world. But it may be said (now that the Jacobinic stage in the women's liberation movement is past) that the accusation cannot be made indiscriminately to all men.

Many were the men, among them the most illustrious in classical antiquity, who spoke to defend woman's virtue and the preeminence of friendship and love between man and woman. Some exposed the apologists of homosexuality as hypocrites who pretended to engage in a superior form of friendship, when in reality they gave free rein to uncontrolled lust. The same reproach that detractors of heterosexuality made to those who did not share their inclination could be turned against themselves. A speaker in Plutarch's *Dialogue on Love* says that boy-love proceeds stealthily and resorts to constant dissembling: "It covers itself with the sand of the wrestling floor, it takes cold baths, it plays the highbrow and publicly proclaims that it is a philosopher and disciplined on the outside—because of the law. But when night comes and all is quiet, *'Sweet is the harvest when the guard's away.'* " If such men ever pursued women it was merely to have children, or to obtain financial gain from the dowry, or to use them in still more dishonorable ways. An example was given by a court jester of Caesar Augustus. The story goes that he observed a powerful man taking undue liberties with his wife during a banquet. He faked being asleep and let his head hang down, as if utterly taken in postprandial slumber. At this point, a slave came into the banquet hall and tried to steal wine from the table. "Damn you!" cried the man, suddenly awake. "I am not asleep for everybody [*non omnibus dormio,* a saying that became proverbial], only for that man." Juvenal gives us to understand that incidents of this kind were not uncommon. With accustomed corrosive sarcasm he says, in the *First Satire:*

> In an age when each pimp of a husband
> Takes gifts from his own wife's lover—if she is
>   barred in law
> From inheriting legacies—and, while they paw each other,
> Tactfully stares at the ceiling, or snores, wide awake, in
>   his wine.

More than a denunciation of the spurious motives of the advocates of pederasty, the egregious men of Greece undertook a mettlesome defense of woman's character, so basely reviled by her ignoble detractors. Plutarch's *Dialogue* ends in a stirring speech that is an admirable eulogy of the beauty of the love that crowns the harmonious relationship between man and wife. Human beings can expect no greater pleasures derived from others, he tells us, than those annexed to this union. Nor is a state more highly esteemed than the enviable one due to Eros: "Nature brings it about that even the gods have need of [this bond]." And yet the existence of learned debates on the merits of homosexuality and the vehemence of the argumentation on either side indicate that a considerable segment of the educated population must have been persuaded that women were not the proper object of the highest form of male affection. The origin of this persuasion, traced to psychological, social, and political roots, is not my concern now. I merely wish to dwell on the known fact that men have nourished a schizoid view of women for a very long time. The idea of woman as simultaneously admirable and despicable goes back to our earliest history and is not, as some seem to suggest, a by-product of Christianity.

The generous words of Christ revealed a new idealism that uplifted the condition of women; even the adulterous woman, who met the most pitiless reproof in all societies, was not excepted from the infinite mercy of Christ. But few men, it seems, took the new teachings into their hearts, and the ambivalent ideas on women persisted after the crumbling of the ancient world's institutions. With this aggravating turn, what had been an unworthy love object was now seen as chief cause of the perdition of men's souls. Intellectual life took refuge in the Church, and this one was infused of a fierce misogynism. Absurd notions were advanced that sought to demonstrate the inferiority of women. Man embodies heat and dryness, it was taught, whereas Woman's fundamental nature is cold and humid. From this composition of the sexes results a hierarchy in biology, in which woman occupies an inferior position relative to man. Woman's inferiority may be seen in anatomical and physiological peculiarities that all can confirm: Her voice is shrill and weaker than that of man; her bones are also weaker; and her cranial vault less capacious and less well-sutured than man's. On the authority of Aristotle's *Historia Animalum* (III, 19), it may be asseverated that, relative to men, women have less blood in their veins. And woman's undistinguished position in the animal kingdom confers upon her a series of

characteristics that men deem contemptible. Unlike other female animals, women have menstruation; they can readily accept the male during pregnancy; and they tend to be delivered
of offspring that carry the imprint of what they have seen,
dreamed of, or eaten during gestation.

Antoninus of Florence concluded that men and women were
separated by so many and so great differences, especially concerning intellect, that it was impossible that they belonged to
the same species. Scholastic philosophers were prompt to
strengthen this conclusion. None other than the revered master, St. Thomas Aquinas, uttered pronouncements adverse to
womanhood, although less radical than those of mystics who,
in their excessive zeal, pushed woman-hatred to pathological
extremes. Aquinas, the supreme expositor of scholasticism,
drew his inspiration from Aristotle, who in turn had established that "small and weak things are accounted as if they
were not" (*Physics* II, 5). Accordingly, women were characterized as having a weak temperament (*Summa Theologica,* question 156, art. 1), and from here it was not too great a leap to
further denigration of the "weaker" sex. Being unstable of
reason and weak of temperament, women are easily led astray.
Therefore, concludes St. Thomas, as regards the body, women
cannot be described as continent.

To reinforce the concept of a fundamental and unbridgeable
chasm separating the two sexes—always to the greater glory
of male superiority—the intellectuals of the Middle Ages de-
lighted in compiling absurd notions that passed for scientific
facts, thus sanctioning male supremacist beliefs. A medieval
collection of these 'observations' has been recently reprinted
in the original Latin.[3] The reader can find there, in the traditional question-and-answer format, the prevailing beliefs on
a number of woman-related subjects, such as: why women,

being cold and humid, may be more libidinous than men; why prostitutes rarely conceive despite frequent coition; why women have menstruation, whereas other female animals do not (example of answer: women are restless, cold, and humid; thus, they generate an excess of superfluous humors; this would lead to excessive passions, of which they are purged by the monthly discharge); why pregnant women crave for unusual foods (in pregnancy menstrual blood is retained that carries "diverse and commingled humors," whose effect is exerted upon the orifices of the stomach, causing the unaccustomed appetite); and why the cadavers of a man and a woman, after drowning, float in different directions, that is, the woman lying supine and the man prone *(mulier submersa inveniatur supina, vir autem pronus)*. From several answers offered to the last question, I gather there was no agreement among the learned. It seems that the distribution of weights, such as those of women's posterior parts and men's generational organs (the latter, as usual, a "weighty" consideration), explains their respective positions while floating. On the other hand, some argue that women's breasts are formed of matter of considerable porosity. The air-containing mammary glands are thus comparable to buoys. Provided with these floating devices, the female cadaver tends to adopt the described posture. *Magister dixit.*

The rampant anti-feminism detected in these writings and many others always imprints on the reader the idea that in the Middle Ages the condition of all women was abjection unmitigated. Credence is usually granted to those who say that women were then regarded as no better than beasts of burden and that Church authorities promoted the idea that "women had no soul." This is clearly an unwarranted generalization. A respected historian, Régine Pernoud, has recently attacked what she terms a gross misconception of our contemporaries.[4] She points out that medieval society often held women in greater esteem than did succeeding centuries. Queens, for instance, were crowned in the great cathedrals during ceremonies that wanted nothing in splendor compared with kingly coronations. Their authority was unquestioned. In contrast, by the seventeenth century it was routine to see the royal mistress possessed of a greater influence in the affairs of the state than the legitimate queen. Deference was paid not only to female aristocrats, since legislation existed that ensured considerable freedom of action to the common woman.

In France, according to Pernoud, it was not medieval society, but those that followed, that reinstituted the absolute power of the *pater familias*. It is common knowledge that the consolidation of despotic patriarchy was achieved later, when the Napoleonic code forced women to take the name of their husbands, raised the legal age of majority, and made it obligatory to obtain the father's consent for marriage. The mentioned medievalist persuasively notes that scholarly achievement by women in the Middle Ages reached heights that would have been unattainable in a society truly repressive of women's aspirations. Women could become renowned erudites, like the abbess of Landsberg; respected theologians, like Gertrude of Helfta; or powerful administrators of religious bodies, like the abbess who presided over the famous abbey of Fontevrault, barely twenty-two years old when elevated to a position that placed her in authority over a religious corporation composed of a large male and female membership. This would have been inconceivable, we must agree, in postfeudal times, allegedly more liberal and enlightened. But where Régine Pernoud loses her patience and sounds a little like the irritated pamphleteer is in the matter of "women having no soul." Had this been the case, she rightly argues, the quoted examples of illustrious achievement within the structure of the Church would have been impossible. Had Church leaders been so atrociously blinded by prejudice as to suppose that women had no soul, the Eucharist would have been denied them. But no one, not even sectarians of a furious anti-clericalism, can justly claim that the Church ever departed from the Christian teaching that women are endowed of an immortal soul, as are men; that they are, therefore, created beings of the same spiritual attributes as men; and that they stand in the eyes of our Savior on a plane of perfect spiritual equality with men.

The perdurability of men's dual vision of women as objects of contempt and reverential awe ought to be plain. During the Middle Ages the dual vision was pushed to dramatic heights: Woman was repository of unwholesome humors, but also a majestic figure. For it was then that Marian devotion raised femininity to a heavenly station. To the conception of a disembodied but nevertheless masculine God in Islam and other religions, Christianity opposed the sweet, beneficent, and feminine figure of the Virgin Mary. Men's schizoid tendency with respect to women reached its dramatic nadir. Women were the source of all ills, the root of dissension, and the occasion for sin in the world. But at the same time a feminine presence commanded the movements of heaven as Mother of God. Intercessor, helper, mediator, and dispenser of justice, she deigned to appear before us to hear the pleas of the disconsolate and the beseeching of the suffering.

The services that Mariolatry rendered to the world in modifying and softening the existing perceptions about women can never be extolled enough. An unconscious image of the awesome, life-giving power of women, the Jungian "archetype of the Great Mother," lives in all men. But this obscure mental image of womanhood was painted almost exclusively in dark colors. It was composed of all the fears and the fear-generated hostility that the masculine mind projected unto the unknown feminine. The fear of castration, which Freud exploited so exhaustively, contributed no small part of the frightening portrait. The orientalist Richard Burton detected it even in biblical writings. He translated Psalm 30:13-15, in which the speaker pleads with the Lord for protection against the menaces of the external world, as containing a reference to "the three insatiables: Earth, Hell, and Parts feminine." The Arabs, whom Burton knew so well and who excluded all feminine elements from the idea of God's essence, condensed the negative views of women in mythical figures, like that of Umm Kulsum, an old procuress of whom it was contended that "for the first thirty years she whored; for the next three decades she pimped for friend and foe; and for the last third of her life, bedridden by age and infirmities, she had a buck-goat and a nanny tied up in her room and solaced herself by contemplating their amorous conflicts."[5]

With very few exceptions, all cultures have spawned their images of a Great Goddess in early historical periods. Beneficial features were sometimes associated to the female deity, mainly fertility and a capacity to renew the germinating cycles of nature. But usually her attributes were disturbing, her power immense, and her energy dangerous. The highest manifestations of spirituality in Hindu philosophical thought—complete absence of desires, perfect contemplative serenity—were male. Lord Siva is passive, still, serene, and supremely wise. The goddess Kali, his consort, is fierce: Her shifting moods translate into calamities for her votaries in the villages. Scholars have noted that all the godlings that preside over diseases in the Hindu pantheon are invariably goddesses.[6] And whereas the work of anthropologists shows that a measure of ambivalence is also detected in the worship of the Virgin Mary, it seems to me that a great civilizing step was accomplished when the image of a chiefly punitive and malevolent goddess, to whom worshippers may attribute passions and "menstrual impurity" (see, for instance, Kolenda's study on the goddess of smallpox in the Indian village of Khalapur, in Uttar Pradesh),[7] was replaced by the image of the Queen of Heaven, with the "sky for her mantle, the stars for a crown," symbol of purity and mercy, with the power to intercede in our behalf with God, her Son.

Despite gradual mellowing of tempers, mollification of customs, and progress of civilization, the situation of women in patriarchal society remained a deplorable one. It is impossible, in the space of this essay, to trace the vicissitudes of women's efforts to correct the fixed and widespread view that nature made women fit to handle domestic affairs and little else, while men should be left to conduct the political and professional affairs of the world by themselves. Until not too long ago, women were considered as existing primarily for the sake of men; their chief function was to cater to the needs of men; and their role in society was primarily a sexual one. Men's most prevalent view of women may be said to have been the view of the owner on a piece of property.

The Present

On the surface, men's views on women never changed more radically in the span of one generation than in ours. I still recall the image of women that the mass media projected in my youth: a curious blend of frailty, aloof grace, and glacial composure. My contemporaries will remember, and the curious can easily confirm, what was the predominant form of representation of women in fashion catalogues, magazines, and advertisements. In all these, Woman sat demure and collected. She was the Dainty Woman: No darting eye, no wanton gaze, no free movements could be expected of her in public. If her eyes were not directed downward, they were inexpressive. Hands folded or holding a bouquet; the torso braced in a quaint posture, as for a formal portrait; and her legs harmoniously disposed in ladylike stance; she was never surprised but in such tranquil attitude. The idea was to sell. But to sell one must not do violence to received opinion, and received opinion defined femininity as gentle and dependent, childlike and innocuously prim.

I do not mean to say that the dual vision had been supplanted by this calm portrait. There was also a lascivious version of the Dainty Woman, which could be found inside the discreet covers of lewd magazines. Already, in my youth, the raunchiest segments of publicity and advertising were trying to push her into the limelight, though with little success. In this version, she became unclothed, alluring, seductive, and fascinating. Interesting to note, however, she seemed available but passive: whether reclining languorously on a sofa, supine on the grass, or prone upon a bed, her very indolence likened her to a harem-bound concubine. One might have said a slave offering herself resignedly to the appetite of the consumer. An unfair deal was transacted in the lickerish spheres of the advertising world, whereby the Dainty Woman surrendered dignity in exchange for attention but not power.

In a very short time, no more than two or three decades, the Dainty Woman, shackled with this triple chain of propriety, stylishness, and passivity, was replaced by her less submissive sister, the New Woman. From the flittering images of television, the pages of magazines, and the oversized likenesses of billboards, the New Woman stares at us today with little regard for stilted convention. She abandons the inscrutable demeanor of the idol for the overt smile, the frown, the scowl, and the unfettered gesture. Clad in a minuscule bikini, she advertises beer or cigarettes, whereas earlier in this century she still risked imprisonment for drinking or smoking, not to mention indecent exposure. Her movements are free to the point of bodily contortion. Indeed, it is rare to open a fashion magazine in which she does not wear trousers or jogging suits, and poses in leg splits and spreads that formerly were thought indecorous as well as physically impossible to womanly conformation. All this prance, strut, grimace, and natural ease are but a statement: the emphatic declaration of independence in which the New Woman solemnly avers that all the former prohibitions are obsolete. Nor does it seem that there is need of a reminder. Last night my television set conveyed the image of the New Woman: a brawny, sweaty female athlete bending her trunk to reach down for the iron bar in a weight-lifting competition. The yammering doll has given way to this grunting amazon who heaves and hauls without taking time off to go powder her nose.

Yet this picture is deceiving. By and large, despite her new assertiveness, woman has not ceased to be the idol. Despite the exaggerated expressivity, her face still hides behind a mask. A daily (or nightly) ritual that consists in the application of foundation, rouge, liquid base, mascara, and so on is still scrupulously observed. True, for a while the New Woman rejected the use of face paint altogether, seeing in it the symbol of her alienation and the visible mark, as it were, of her debased condition. But by degrees she persuaded herself that the use of facial decoration was not wholly contemptible and that it made her "look better." And by degrees she relapsed again into the use of tweezers, brushes, pencils, and shadows; and did so with an enthusiasm that ranged between the absurd extreme ridiculed by Callicratides and a most timid approach to cosmetology. In any case, no woman, apart from militant feminist sectarians or the exceptionally strong of character, would dare today to display a wan, unpainted face in a world where millions of her properly made-up sisters flaunt their beautician's know-how.

Like her timorous predecessor, the New Woman has sanctioned Baudelaire's claim that "woman's right, and even her duty, is to apply herself to appear magical and supernatural; she must dazzle, she must charm; as an idol, she must gild herself to be worshipped."[8] In vain, then, does she protest that she does not wish to be worshipped. An idol that speaks is a supernatural phenomenon that in itself commands reverential awe. It is useless for her to say that she longs for a less exalted and more equal condition; that she aspires not to homage, but to companionship and respect. These protestations are uttered by an icon or a statue. For, to quote Baudelaire once more, "who does not see that facial makeup aims to expunge the stains that nature had outrageously sown therein, and to create an abstract unity in the grain and hue of the skin, which unity, like that produced by a dancer's leotard, immediately approaches the human being of the statue, that is to say, of a divine and superior being?"

The idol, like the statue, belongs in a different order of things: that of symbols, and dreams, and derivative representations of reality. Note that the professed aim of facial makeup is beauty. The pithy reality of a human face is systematically destroyed in order to make it appealing, that is to say, attractive or seductive. But seduction is entirely a matter of induced trance or hypnosis. It is creative mirage; it is a game of pretense. This is why facial makeup has been called "a pretense for a pretense," which Baudrillard[9] compared to a double dupery, or reflexive deceit: not just like the antics of a male transvestite who deceives us by pretending to be a woman; rather, like a woman who poses as a male transvestite—a helicoidal deceit, whose fascination consists in that it moves us from one illusion to another, and back again to the original deceit.

Contradictions are everywhere visible in the New Woman. Consider one of them, engagingly outlined by Susan Brownmiller, a perceptive writer.[10] It is the attire of the "successful woman," the one who is generally thought closest to attaining the ideal of parity of the sexes. If she has climbed to the highest spheres of the corporate world, she covers her trunk with a jacket. It would be a serious hindrance to professional upward mobility to accentuate an all-too-feminine bustline, as with a tight yellow sweater or a revealing décolletage. No woman who aspired to enter the executive room—other than as an underling leered at with impunity by her male superiors—ever dared to incur such sartorial indiscretions. Thus, her upper body is covered with a jacket, indistinguishable from the male garment. Below the waist, however, corporate officialdom permits a woman's skirt that terminates above the knee. Here, femaleness is given safe-conduct: The legs are exposed, and their sexual appeal not just left undisturbed but triumphantly, unabashedly enhanced by the silky sheen of stockings and the use of unhealthy, torturing high-heeled shoes designed to accentuate the legs' smooth contour. Such the schizoid split of women's fashion in the exalted executive spheres of the Western world: upper asceticism and lower sensuality, much like the Greek partition of the body, described in *Timaeus,* into spiritual and animal domains divided by the sheet of the diaphragm.

It is only the callous and unperceptive who attribute these absurd contradictions to woman's unthinking frivolity or vanity. The truth is that she moves today, as in the past, in an absurd world that racks her with contrary pressures. In her relations with men, the New Woman is not exempt of the need to attract and repel, and to constantly toe the precarious line between the desire to entice and the need to repulse. In vain do we tell ourselves that she lives in an era of "new openness," in which all commerce between the sexes can at last take place free of hypocrisy and pretense. In the large urban centers, where this shibboleth passes unquestioned, is precisely where the contradiction is greatest. It is here where the opportunities for male aggression are multiplied, and the occasions for female diffidence increased accordingly. Here, in these nuclei of social progress, in these beachheads of liberality, a woman must be constantly on her guard. She must rid herself of insistent followers and learn to discern a shy suitor from a potential attacker who watches her in ambush. She must avoid a male presence in dark alleys, deserted lots, solitary elevators, or unwatched buildings. She must protect herself from deviant males who press themselves against her in crowded places, trains, or buses, deriving a sickly, vicarious pleasure from the anonymous contact. When a disturbing ambiguity of solicitations and potential threats constantly surrounds her, is it a wonder that instead of the vulnerable expressivity of a human face, she prefers the inalterable demeanor of a mask?

Among the external determinants of her behavior and not the least of the ills that beset the New Woman is male antifeminism. In its simple form, this sentiment is but a remnant of the old view of women as male property. It is the persistent sentiment, voiced by the ancients and in unbroken line by all male generations down to the present, that it is unwise for a man to expect solace from wariness in the company of women. That to support one is hard, but to put up with a self-supporting one is torture. That if she be ugly, it is annoying to live with her; but if comely, an anxious distraction to keep her. That if she be worthy and admirable, a man's troubles shall increase, for he must share her groans when in pain and her misery when dejected; but if vile, there is no glory in having what no man would possibly covet.

Deeper than all these banal commonplaces, however, is a fundamental, deep-seated male antieroticism, and hence antifeminism. It is the inarticulated feeling that the erotic is draining, enervating, and deleterious to man's worthy accomplishment. It is no longer the blanket antieroticism of a St. Jerome, who owned that "it is disgraceful to love another man's wife at all, or one's own too much." Rather, the more civilized, contemporary expression is an injunction to halt, decelerate, dilute, or 'sublimate' the erotic impulse. It is a formulation of today's male intelligentsia that the erotic must be opposed. Modern science acknowledges the role of erotic life as source and first motor of much of our behavior. But men also know and fear its potential disruptive effect. Aldous Huxley compared the erotic impulse to the turbine that propels the aircraft, that is, the human spirit. Without the resistance of the air, the vessel would never take off; no matter how powerful its engine, it would not lift off in a vacuum. And so it is with man's erotic life in the Huxleian view: Only through antagonism, or the opposition of the forward erotic drive and its unceasing repression, shall the male spirit soar.

If there is a constant in men's views on women, it is duality and ambiguity. Only the tone has changed. Woman is no longer condemned in the grandiloquent style of moralists of yore nor eulogized in the fustian manner of her past defenders—although, in truth, the two could not always be distinguished from each other. Instead, with terms borrowed from scientific disciplines, the sages of today give new voice to the old ambivalence. Woman still represents the embodiment of a life-force that is at one time intense, redeeming, dangerous, and awful. Something that cannot be avoided, but must be dealt with by vague systems of indulgence and prohibition. No one can tell, however, when to yield and when to oppose; and no one presumes to tell us how to achieve the optimal combination.

THE CONDITIONS FOR
SEDUCTION, ACCORDING TO
AN OLD CHINESE TEXT

Chinese culture lacks a tradition of "great seducers." We find no Don Juans or Casanovas among the eminently practical inhabitants of the Middle Kingdom. As far as I know there is nothing strictly comparable to those illustrious philanderers in the five times millenarian literature of China. All the more remarkable, then, that one of the most perceptive accounts of seduction—engagingly narrated and almost clinical in its detached observation—should be owed to a Chinese novelist. It appears in an ancient work entitled "On the Water's Edge," written toward the end of the Yuan dynasty (the fourteenth century of our era) by Shi Nai-an.

The episode refers to a young man inflamed with desire for a married woman, the wife of a baker who ekes out a meager living selling his bread on the streets. As in the West in times past, the young man must solicit the intercession of a go-between, indispensable element to amorous intrigue: useless to attempt anything without this intervention. The go-between, Mrs. Wang, listens to the young man's plight and is made aware of his intentions. She answers with a prefatory systematization of the requirements that, in her judgment, must be met by any man expecting success in erotic enterprise:

"First, you must have the looks of Pan-An [a strikingly handsome man who, according to Chinese historians, lived during the Jin dynasty]. Second, you must have a donkey's endowment [this shocking requirement, expressed with no further qualification in the Chinese text, may refer generally to lustful vigor capable of prompting an unflagging pursuit, or, perhaps, it simply means just what it says. The reader would do well to remember that it is a Chinese peasant who speaks, whose direct knowledge of life is expressed through equally direct, earthy language]. Third, you must have the riches of Deng Tong [favorite of Wen Di (179-157 B.C.), emperor of the Han dynasty. An astrologer, after looking at the lines around his mouth, predicted that he would die of hunger. The emperor wished to prevent this calamity, and granted rich mining concessions to his friend. Deng Tong was in charge of minting coins in Szechwan, with unrestricted leave to delve into the national treasury. He accumulated an immense fortune. Emperor Wen passed away, his favorite fell into disgrace under the successor, was imprisoned, and died, as predicted, of starvation].[1] Fourth, you must have great patience. You must be capable of appearing humble even when you think you have been affronted. The fifth and last requirement is leisure. You must have the time to plan, then to follow your strategy, whatever this may be. You must always be available when required."

After the presentation of this succinct list of conditions for a well-turned-out seduction, the young man rejoins that he feels himself equal to the challenge. He is aware that the old woman is probably setting forth a list of stipulations difficult to meet in order to eliminate the idle and the insecure and leave only the serious customer to transact with. Thus, the young man represents to her that he can meet the requirements in a satisfactory way. As to the first one, he is not exceptionally handsome, but he is young and not without some attractiveness. As to the second requirement, he cannot brag about being a worthy rival of the donkey, whose volumetric proportions are proverbial throughout the world. Rather, to keep discourse at the level of the zoological metaphors used by Mrs. Wang, he compares himself to the turtle. This animal has a long and flexuous neck that terminates in a bulbous head; aside from its biologic significance, this conformation carries a rich symbolism in Asiatic folklore. The third requirement the young man cannot meet: The riches of Deng Tong are not his. But whatever property he has is more secure than the sadly evanescent fortune of Deng Tong, the ill-starred favorite, and, adds the young man, more readily available to those who wish to serve him. The fact is, he has enough money to give him the needed leisure, thus satisfying the third and fifth requirements. As to the fourth one, a humble and patient nature, could there be any doubt of his willingness to face labors and difficulties, since he has come asking for help after many sleepless nights and is pained by all the symptoms of love sickness?

An understanding is thus reached. Having agreed on the feasibility of the enterprise, the go-between is ready to outline the recommended strategy. It is formulated by Mrs. Wang in the following speech:

"The woman you desire is my neighbor. I know her for a good seamstress; she cuts and embroiders her own clothes.

This is what we will do. First, you bring me several rolls of good silk, fine thread to be used in embroidering, and fancy lace. Then, I go to her house and invite her for tea at my place. I will say that a rich gentleman has taken pity on me, an old woman, and has given me the materials I needed to prepare my own funeral clothes. I am going to die soon, and, save for the generosity of this man—may he be ten thousand times blessed!—I would have gone to the last voyage dressed like a beggar. Now, at last, I no longer have to meet my dead ancestors in the garb of a miser. A fine robe, a magnificent one, indeed, they are going to see me in! Now, I will say to her, all I am afraid of is not being able to finish the dress on time. For the astrologer that I consulted assures me that the dress must be started and completed within a few auspicious days. And how am I, a shaky old woman who must squint at every stitch, going to complete the task in such a brief span of time? When I am through telling her all this, I expect, if I know her well, that she will volunteer to help me. And if she volunteers, let me tell you this: you have ten percent of your desire already in your pocket.

"Of course, she may volunteer to do the work in her own house, not in mine. In that case, you might as well forget it; you have lost. But if she agrees to come to do it at my house, you can count with twenty percent of your desire.

"The work will take several days. It is the first two or three days that are crucial to your project. I will talk about you in flattering terms. If she decides, after two days, that she has helped me enough and wishes to go home, then you might as well forget it: you've lost. But if she stays for the third day, you have won thirty percent of the prize.

"On the afternoon of the third day you appear at my house, dressed for the occasion. You stroll casually, in your elegant clothes. You stop at the threshold of my door, looking your best, and you cough discreetly. Then you say in a loud voice: 'Dear Mrs. Wang! I haven't seen you in a long time! How have you been?' I have been ready waiting for you, and I invite you in. If the minute she sees you she stands up in a hurry and leaves, then you might as well forget it: you've lost. However, if she stays sitting at her working table, and does not show that she is about to leave, then you have a forty-percent victory.

"In our conversation I will praise your wealth and your achievements. You will praise her embroidery work. Be quite emphatic in your praise, and let's see what happens next. If she stays generally demure, hardly answering, there is no sense in persisting: you've lost. But if she answers your praise, especially if she seems animated in her answers, you have gone fifty percent of the way.

"We are now in midstream. What we do next is as follows. I will say how lucky it is for me to have been given the fine materials for my funeral robe; and how lucky to have found this good woman who is helping me with the design and actual sewing of this garment. Having said this, I will find it easy to say that it must be a very good day for me, since I am blessed to have both of my benefactors simultaneously under my roof. Such an auspicious juncture surely calls for celebration. You readily agree, and offer to give me money to go buy some wine, and some food. If the minute she hears of this plan she says she really must go, then you might as well forget it: you've lost. But if she stays over while all these preparations are going on, consider her sixty percent yours.

"At this point you must observe her reactions carefully. I take your money, make for the door, and try to find occasion to tell her, on my way out: 'I would be obliged to see you entertain this kind gentleman. See to it that he is not bored, and try to keep him happy while I'm gone.' If she makes excuses and wants to leave, the game is over: you have lost. But if she takes this with alacrity, she is seventy percent yours.

"After I come back with the food and wine, I set the table, then ask her to put down her work, if she still insists on her sewing. Speaking to her aside, I will tell her that this is her chance to be in the good graces of a charming, generous, and good-hearted man. I will say that she ought to profit from the occasion, and make merry with us at your expense. I will insist on how great is your liberality, and how excellent the viands and wine that I have bought with your money. Mark very well how she acts at this point. She may decide to take some food while sitting away from us, on her own table. In that case, there is no more to be done, for you have lost. But if she approaches us, and sits with you, and sounds jovial and merry, you have, I think, an eighty-percent triumph.

"At the peak of the merriment, when I see that her cheeks are flushed and her eyes are shiny, and the conversation is most lively and enjoyable, I will pretend that there is no more wine. I will say that I am going out to bring some more, but that it will take much longer this time, because the supply at the local store has been exhausted and I must go farther. I will make it obvious that I am locking the door behind me. Let us watch attentively what her reaction is then. If one of anxiousness and immediate preparation to leave the place, it is defeat: you lost. But if she stays, seemingly unconcerned about the present turn of developments, this is almost a victory—ninety percent.

"You are almost there. Now you tell her some sweet words. Go easy now; not too anxious. You do not touch her right away; you do not rush to her. The conversation is sweet, and already on the personal level. The atmosphere is cozy and inviting. You are eating together, very close to each other. You have placed your chopsticks very close to the edge of the table. You pretend that, with an unintentional movement, a gesture of your arm to punctuate the conversation, you have pushed the chopsticks to the floor with the wide sleeves of your robe. You bend to pick them up, but instead of going for the chopsticks you go for the lady's small feet, enclosed in finely embroidered silk shoes, which you squeeze lovingly in your hands. And what she does then is the final test. She may rise, indignant, from the table. She may scream bloody hell, in which case I must rush in to her aid, since I am waiting outside, and have not gone anywhere. Pity. You came thus far, yet you lost. But if she doesn't, mind you, if she doesn't, that is one hundred percent. She's yours. You may take her."[2]

The plan takes place exactly as the go-between had predicted. The description of its blow-by-blow accomplishment is a masterpiece of oriental *verismo*. So is its language, which compels us to make some clarifications. In particular, the second requirement of Mrs. Wang's list deserves some comment. Its bold formulation in the Chinese text may offend some readers, but this need not be so. An early, naturalistic stage of cultural development invariably links organ size to functional proficiency: all-seeing demigods are represented with huge, often multiple eyes; the iconography of an acute sense of hearing calls for long, mobile ears, like those of some animals; a swift stride is associated with long, strong legs. Before the subtle interplay of mind and male sexuality became fully appreciated, nothing seemed plainer than the complete subordination of the latter to genitalic size. The prototype seducer thus appeared as an individual afflicted with what is called, in medical terms, *macrogenitosomia*. His potency, today traced to factors that range from physiologic to sociologic, was then assigned a strictly genital seat. Survival of these notions among the peasantry of China was perfectly natural; and it was a masterful stroke of Shi Nai-an to have placed its expression in the mouth of the old go-between. Nor is this the only allusion of its kind among Chinese writers of old times. In the *Stories of East Chou's Many States* by Yu Xiao-yu, the story is told of a man who rose to ill-fated prominence by the sheer strength of his erectile tissue.

During the childhood of Emperor Shi Huang Di (then prince of Qin), his widowed mother saw fit to take Prime Minister Lu as a lover. This timorous man, however, fell short— in more ways than one—of the royal expectations. Lu feared the time when the young prince, jealous of his power, would reclaim his rightful authority and speed up a bloody day of reckoning. Wishing to avert the charge of usurpation of power, to which he was liable for having unlawfully shared the royal bed, he contrived to find a substitute for his own mediocre presence in the nuptial chamber. He found the right substitute in Lao Ai, a vulgar, uneducated man whom the prime minister expected to manipulate at will. Lao Ai lacked the social graces indispensable for advancement in a refined court. He made his living in the market and could no more be expected to show wit or delicacy of manners than a courtier to match his strength at hauling bales of fodder or his skill at telling the good from the bad cabbages. But if he was lacking in such acquirements, he was oversupplied with other, more natural endowments. Let us say, euphemistically, that Mrs. Wang's second require-ment presented no embarrassment to Lao Ai: He had enough to spare. Conscious of this superiority, he was not above using exhibitionism for the purpose of self-promotion. It was this lack of restraint that caused his meteoric ascent and his ruinous end.

A festivity took place in the town, in celebration of the harvest. The townspeople assembled in the marketplace to watch the entertainment. Amid music and revelry, the turn came for acrobats and their shows of muscular dexterity. It was then that the spectators were regaled with an astonishing prowess, the likes of which had not registered in the townspeople's recent or remote memory. Lao Ai came on the stage. Assistants brought a heavy wooden wheel from a cart. Into the spaces between the thick spokes, he inserted that part of his anatomy on which hinged his reputation and rested his pride. The assistants made the heavy wheel turn, imparting to it a fast circular motion. Lao Ai, with no more support than his vaunted *corpora cavernosa,* brought the ponderous wheel to a stop.

One might have said a child staying a gyrating whirligig with his finger, so easy did Lao Ai make it appear. He might have smiled in triumph, as one who boastfully announces: "Look: no hands!" for the amazement of the populace. He then showed that the astonishing feat had caused him no hurt. The crowd broke out into laughter and spontaneous applause.

Talk of his prowess spread far and wide. Prime Minister Lu, perhaps well informed of the queen's tastes and inclinations, praised Lao Ai's unexampled vigor. She was intrigued and wished to meet him. Lao Ai's unique endurance was subjected to a further test (this time not in public, and with the queen for sole judge), from which he emerged much in the royal favor. A way was found to introduce him into the royal household without raising eyebrows. Guards seized him and publicly announced that he would henceforward be made a eunuch in the service of the queen. To further impress this change of status on the minds of the people, an animal (a donkey, of course) was castrated, and its severed, bloodied male appendage conspicuously displayed on the pretense that it had belonged to Lao Ai. In the course of several years the false eunuch managed to procreate two children with the queen. Nor was it difficult to conceal gestation and birth from a people so gullible as to have stood ignorant of the previous deceit. By this time, however, the prince had come of age. When Shi Huang Di assumed the reins of power, authority found in him an able steward and a redoubtable despot. He uncovered the intrigue and punished the guilty parties with merciless rigor. Lao Ai was put to death by dismemberment. The queen mother was imprisoned and would have met as cruel an end but for the tenacity with which the Chinese have ever clung to the virtue of filial piety. Floods, plagues, and other disasters ravaged the land, and a comet coursed the skies presaging yet worse ills. Astrologers were unanimous in attributing these prodigies and calamities to the unfilial conduct of the ruler, who was thus pressured into releasing his mother. The ire of the elements then relented, and in the relative calm that followed Shi Huang Di rose to magnificence never equalled in China or elsewhere. Our own age caught a glimpse of this awesome splendor when, in 1974, archaeologists discovered his tomb, surrounded by a subterranean maze in which seven thousand life-sized terra cotta sculptures of horses and soldiers formed the emperor's last guard: a spectacle whose uncanny realism and formidable proportions stagger the imagination.

East is East and West is West! In our part of the world, the young at heart vibrate with emotion at the prowesses of medieval knights, in tales by Sir Walter Scott. Clad in burnished armor and displaying the colors of his lady, many a gallant knight conquered the dame's haughty heart with his skill in tilting at the ring. But nowhere in the West do we hear of a paladin who tilted, like Lao Ai, with his own, natural spear. Absurd, you say? Not entirely. Considering the intent of jousting and the ultimate purpose of the toils and pains of the champions, it seems to me that the original oriental innovation is not devoid of internal logic.

Later times saw a progressive sophistication in the ways to evaluate the relative worth of male genital anatomy in seduction. The Chinese, who had been so partial in their emphasis on measurements, were also first to realize the irrelevance of using the yardstick. The cruel practice of creating eunuchs showed them that the resolute make do with less than the apportionment of nature. They entrusted the custody of the emperors' harems to those unfortunates whom they made men "minus the peccant part," as the orientalist Richard Burton says referring to the equivalent métier among the Arabs. But despite the atrocious mutilation, seductions went on. The seducer availed himself of whatever remnant the ferocity of his captors had spared; if none, technical ingeniosity took the place of the missing wherewithal. From this, we are forced to conclude that mind is preeminent over matter, and that seduction's second requisite is the commodity most widely available to men; it is, to their misfortune, much more abundant than common sense—which Descartes, with unbelievable optimism, declared in his *First Meditation* to be men's most prevalent characteristic.

The third condition is riches, and being not afraid to give them away. There is nothing uniquely oriental in this requirement, but the contemporary debate over its significance invites comment. For it is said to be natural for man to be gift-giver, and for woman to grant sexual access in return.

Anthropologists seem to agree with the popular notion. Donald Symons examines this question in a recent book.[3] In theory, male seductive persuasion, as shown by courtship behavior in primitive societies, could correspond to any one of the following possibilities: *(a)* only men give gifts; *(b)* men and women exchange gifts, but men's are always of higher value; *(c)* an exchange of gifts takes place, but there is no mention of relative values; *(d)* women's gifts are always of greater value; and *(e)* only women give gifts. Symons concludes that no examples of the last two possibilities have been scientifically documented in the specialized literature. Research in anthropology demonstrates that the majority of preliteral societies conform to patterns *(a)* and *(b);* a few reports allude to *(c),* but no valid documentation exists to this day of preliteral societies adhering to patterns *(d)* and *(e).*

Thus, the rule has been to make men pay. And this cannot be a corruption of mores contingent upon the moral dissolution of modern civilization, since males "in a state of nature" are equally subject to the tribute. But this does not mean that this state of affairs is "normal," or that it must be fatalistically accepted as biological destiny. An alternative explanation is that the subjection of women, a widespread and well-entrenched phenomenon, has forced them to wrest power from men's control by hook or by crook; and they found it most expedient to do it by bartering. A corollary of this argument is that when the emancipation of women is complete, the marketplace analogy will disappear. On the other hand, it is impossible to ignore the universality and perdurability of the marketplace analogy in male-female relationships. If men have always been willing to pay, and women advantageously to negotiate, it may be that something in their respective biologic constitutions predisposes them to enter into precisely this sort of arrangement. In the eighteenth century, Diderot commiserated over the state of women by saying that "the only thing that is taught them is how to wear the fig leaf that they received from their first grandmother. All that is repeated to them for eighteen or nineteen years in a row is this: "My daughter, watch your fig leaf; your fig leaf sits well, your fig leaf sits badly." It may be significant that today, when social conditions are much changed, Symons can still entitle a chapter of his book devoted to this problem "Copulation as a Female Service" and use by way of epigraph this quotation from a male personage in a novel by Saul Bellow: "I never touched a fig leaf that did not turn into a price tag."

Niggardliness rarely prevails over lust, although Aulus Gellus has it, in *Attic Nights,* that this occurred to an aging Demosthenes. When told what amount of money would secure for him the favors of a courtesan he much desired, he answered: "I will not buy repentance for ten drachmas." The rule is otherwise for most men. In them, the consumer's "credit mentality" habitually reigns: Enjoy now, and pay later. E. S. Turner, in his engrossing and erudite *History of Courting,* relates the plight of a disappointed young lover who kept a record of the expenses he incurred in courting. That he saw fit to keep the accounting already shows he was no squanderer. Nevertheless, he had occasion to compare his own notes with old entries of similar nature in his father's yellowing diary (a compulsion for bookkeeping ran in the family), and thus confirmed that the cost for such things as flowers, telegrams, Valentine cards, tickets for shows, and boxes of chocolates had risen many times in the span of one generation. Alarmed at the money drain that seemed so far ahead of inflation, he complained in an open letter published by an American magazine: "I must say that the conversation, entertainment, and mental companionship that I have received in return for these $1000 a year seem to me to be priced beyond their real value."[4]

Coda

Seduction ought to be the subject of perpetual wonderment. Consider the attending circumstances. A man and a woman approach each other. They are, relatively speaking, strangers. They may be mutually acquainted, but that is all. To suppose that an affectionate bond already exists between them is to destroy the possibility of seduction. For the latter to exist at all, mutuality of sentiment between the participants must be absent; if this is present we must speak of courting or something else, but not seduction. It occurs, then, that in one of the participants—the seducer—germinates an interest in altering the consciousness of the other in such a way that the latter feels compelled to give herself or himself to the former. Can anyone imagine a more peculiar appetency? Nor is it ever clear how this desire arises in the first place. The seducer is somehow struck by the presence of the other or by an element that in some way relates to this alien presence. The attention of the seducer must first be trapped, that is, he or she must first be seduced. But this is not the most remarkable aspect of the relationship. Note that the motivation of the seducer may derive from any point of the moral spectrum, from the saintly to the infernal. He or she may be inspired by the purest love and compelled to seek union with the beloved for altruistic reasons. On the other hand, the actuating principle may be conceit, sensuality, revenge, or love of money. And the astonishing fact is that regardless of the motives, the external form of seduction remains the same. To fix the attention of the seduced, all seducers must bring the same dialectic to bear:

declarations, protestations, oaths, shows of devotion, and so on. A purely phenomenological approach is worthless: sincerity and insincerity *appear* the same.

Two unknown values, therefore, complicate the equation of seduction: sincerity and dissembling. And these two terms account for the most hurtful abrasions of both the masculine and feminine sensibilities. Consider one scenario, well known to many an adolescent male. A girl is idealized and cherished: For her sake, no proof of devotion seems excessive, no demand unreasonable. The veneration usually courses in silence. When she comes close to her worshipper, this one seems to be seized by paralysis, stammers, and generally appears maladroit. Time consolidates her power over his susceptible soul. His heart fills with chivalric dreams of loving happiness. He conceives wild expectations of everlasting bliss. So high has he raised the pedestal on which he placed her that she becomes a celestial queen. No wonder that in her presence he is overawed: Heavenly majesty leaves mortal men dumbstruck.

But, lo and behold! One day, an unworthy wight, a carefree rascal, approaches her throne, and to the worshipper's utter dismay, takes the idol away with not so much as a trace of reverence or respect. What is still more unbearable, the queen in her glory seems to be enjoying the proceedings immensely. To all appearances, the vulgar fellow amuses her. He delights her. Seemingly, she does not mind his baseness or his insincerity. And she reserves not one thought for the disappointed worshipper, who now bleeds at her feet, unable to recover from the double blow of seeing the triumph of a rival who does not deserve her—or so he thinks—and learning that rapturous love is no guarantee for winning favor.

This experience is men's first and most effective lesson in cynicism. A woman, goes the lesson, is apt to fall for what is purely dazzling and superficial. The vulgar playboy, unhampered by timidity and deft in the wiles that ensnare women's hearts, stands a much higher chance to be successful in love than the sincere, devoted, but clumsy suitor. This lesson must not be easily forgotten: that neither depth of feeling nor personal worth count for much in women's estimation. He who aspires to their love must first learn the techniques of seduction, which call, above all, for theatrical aptitude, dissembling, and simulation. The conclusion of our disillusioned young man is that seduction is a craft, or a game that may be mastered, provided that one keeps one's self-command and develops the appropriate strategies, methods, and cunningness. In other words, provided that insincerity rules the systematic pursuit.

On the feminine side the situation is worse, since it is compounded by the tradition of passivity annexed to womanly deportment. Too direct an allurement would be counterproductive: It is not ladylike to be overly inviting. Incitements must be carefully monitored lest they become brash and therefore discrediting. It is no use to argue that the new parity of the sexes has reversed traditional roles or modified former courting behavior. The majority of women still live under countless pressures and external impositions that render impossible the freedom of expression that men have enjoyed in their dealings with the opposite sex. In greater or lesser measure, the feminine stance of seduction is still characterized by passivity, real or contrived. It is properly symbolized in the fairy tale of Sleeping Beauty, who awaits the passing prince, as Susan Brownmiller so graphically puts it, "while in a state of suspended animation," and lying horizontally on a bier-like bed. The prince stops by, reclines over the supine maiden— the sexual symbolism could not be clearer—and breathes new life into her with a kiss, just as Ezekiel (37:9) restored life and flesh to a heap of dry bones with the sole aid of the wind.

But what if the prince chose not to stop by Sleeping Beauty's tower? Would she be left to sleep forever amid the spiderwebs that hang from the beamed ceiling to her counterpane? How to call him, how to attract his attention without altering graceful poise and collected demeanor? Like the timid male lover who sees his love object swept away by undeserving but self-confident vulgarity, the female lover pines away at the sight of her beloved in the hands of uninhibited, shameless women. Her torment, however, is greater. She suffers from the sense of loss and from hopelessness, for she realizes her impotence to struggle against misfortune. Moreover, she sees the futility in trying to enlighten the reckless swain. He is too thick and unperceptive. He fails to see that an ambitious, evil woman has made him the toy of her wanton whims or a mere pawn in her scheming. And from this whole affair emerges the feminine version of the untrustworthiness of the opposite sex: men are breezy, unforeseeing, reckless, and inconsiderate. They are easily baited by sex, which overrides in them any consideration of sobriety and mature deliberation. Lacking in foresight and prompt to follow the urgings of their instincts, men's nature partakes of childish immaturity and brutish animality. They are "big children," says the women's commonplace. At any rate, a cunningly calculating approach works best with them. Rarely can they be dealt with by an aboveboard, straightforward attitude, and almost never so in amorous affairs, not to mention the fact that openness in these matters may clash with officially sanctioned canons of feminine conduct. Titillation, suggestion, and various forms of manipulation have been historically the best methods. Lastly, seduction is manipulation, a craft whose techniques may be learned, and at which many women are exceptionally gifted.

When the two participants are so imbued of the notion that seduction is a game of skill and astuteness, it comes as no surprise that its development often strikes the observer as consisting of a match in which two adversary wits are squared against each other. The spectator's inclination is to ask: Who will win? But to this question there can be no easy answer since the end of the game is not obvious. Not the least of the paradoxes is that the two contenders entertain different opinions as to the aim of the game in which they are passionately involved.

In the first place, for some seducers the game may have no object outside itself. It is possible that some deviant men, as well as rare women, may feel that the end of seduction is to seduce. Of the myriad interpretations of the mythical figure of Don Juan, this one—that the archetype-seducer focuses his interest wholly upon the seduction process itself—may be the least attractive to the artist or to the imaginative and refined, but is definitely the most plausible to the clinically minded. The determinant mental mechanisms are seen most clearly in the gambler, a being who may be thought of as instancing a different expression of the same basic disorder. For the gambler, the stakes are relatively unimportant: They are the pretext of the game, but not its object. The end of the game is to play. All else is secondary. The fascination resides in those magical moments when the dice are rolling or the roulette is spinning, and the soul is suspended, and time is stopped, and the whole of reality suddenly is charged of a different, provisional meaning. This is what matters. Ask any true gambler. He will tell you that it matters more than life, since life itself may be thrown in, just like any other bet, atop the green carpet. "If the end of the game were to win," wrote Baudrillard, "then the best player would be the one who cheats." But to cheat is to destroy the fascination. Accordingly, the mythical Don Juan does not cheat. He is the personification of sincerity in the sense that all his acts accord with his professed purpose. But this transparent consistency is at odds with society. His enormous success, partly owed to his sincerity, aims at goals that are not the goals of the seduced. Moreover, his goals are labile, transient, and evanescent; they are immediately fulfilled and must perpetually be renewed elsewhere after each conquest.

Some seducers could not be classified as sensualists, since they would not trade immaterial rewards derived from a seduction in process, whatever these may be, for the physical enjoyment that the achieved seduction makes possible. But it would be hypocritical or blind to deny that sensualism underlies most of the masculine seducing activity that takes place in the world. The male is commonly of the opinion that the prize is sexual engagement. To win is to bed. Once copulation has been achieved, the game is over. He has "scored," as he puts it, using as much crassitude as naiveté in this typically male saying. He can now dismantle the edifice of craftiness that he so painstakingly built, or maintain it for as long as he deems it practical, without altering his definition of victory.

The female is not so coarse. Women have yet to divest themselves of the deeply ingrained conviction that the end of seduction is to inspire love. Not that they have not tried. In recent years, the feminist movement has questioned the traditional views of male and female eroticism. Just as militant feminists have tried to suffuse a measure of femininity into the male personality, so, too, some women have tried to adopt what passes for the male model of eroticism. In the masculine capacity for unlimited physical pleasure *without* need to commit their hearts, they have seen a kind of triumphant free-dom. They have wished to imitate it. And, save for rare, suspect exceptions, they have lost.

Not that their attempt was wanting in resolve. In Erica Jong's novels, the sexual act becomes "zipless": a deliberate experiment to be like men. Anaïs Nin's confessions detail the same undaunted effort to attain the untrammeled mastery of the senses. Bewilderment or disgust emerges from the promis-cuous experience. In Jong's *Parachutes and Kisses,* the protag-onist, Isadora, engages numerous men in her obsessive search for the masculine model of eroticism. She cannot bring herself to spend the whole night with any of them. She is seized with an invincible disgust for those "unknown bodies" that lie by her side. It occurs to her to actually push them out the door, to send them home from her apartment at 3:00 in the morning. Biologic predetermination, or centuries of learned behavior? Diderot may have shown stunning prescience when, in 1772, he wrote in his essay on women: "Our organ is more indulgent. . . . Sovereign [physical] happiness escapes women while in the arms of the man they adore. We find it easily in the embrace of a complacent woman whom we loathe." Whether the dif-ference in sensibilities is constitutional or acquired, I defy the sages to tell us. If it is the result of inveterate social pressures, it will disappear one day. But it will not be soon.

Not bedding, but "a relationship," is what women seek. And in this difference it is impossible to fail to acknowledge a distinct superiority of the feminine sensibility, however cant-ish this may sound. Whereas men are overwhelmed by the strong pulsations of the body, women remain free to bestow a wider meaning to the corporeal elements of the erotic. The erotic does not end in spastic contractions and reflex dis-charges; it transcends them, to reach into the ethereal realms of memory and feeling, like a note that reverberates long after the string was pulsated. Woman may resort to her body in ways congruous with her aims and in a fashion is apt to be ranked as "manipulative." But only when she is long remembered and continually desired, as if by a cyclically renewed, ever rekindled thirst; only when her image fills to capacity the consciousness of the man she has chosen, and stretches temporally beyond the meager boundaries of physiologic immediacy; only then does she claim to have won. When her immanent presence projects across time and space to leave a profound impress on another being: *then* she has "scored."

VIEWS ON THE EROTIC

Some go through life unmoved by its cataclysms. It is possible to ignore destitution, exposure, misery, and infirmity. It is even possible to be persuaded, as are mystics, that all is dream, vanity, or illusion. But no one remains indifferent to the power of erotic passion. Few things in life produce reactions as diverse; none as deep or as lasting. Equable judgments are rarely to be heard. Some speak of the erotic with cynicism, others with excitement, still others with nostalgia, and few with fear. Yet fear of the erotic would be easiest to understand. For when we see that an epidemic is upon us, and that all around us there is random decimation, and that now on our left, now on our right, bodies fall grievously smitten, prudence would advise to tread cautiously, and to flee the place with all dispatch.

The malady is a sort of wave that rolls the sexes against each other. It starts as a desire of not negligible intensity, but of prompt subsidence and easy satisfaction. *Lust* is a fine word, redolent of the notions of desire, yearning, and tense anticipation. But out of this sentiment, for which moralists have nothing but censure, may arise an obsession, a monomania that thrives in the profoundest regions of our sensible being. Stendhal called it *amour-passion,* using a double appellative, after the fashion of Linnaeus for naming the living creatures. Men under its sway evince the full range of symptoms of an intoxication: Perceptions are effaced; the scale of spiritual values is toppled; and the most sober spirits, or the most settled minds, respond with childish reasonings to the objections raised by prudence against the assuagement of desire.

In sum, a surfeit of venereal matters wreaks havoc in the mind. This is why eroticism was ever condemned in the West. Greco-Roman thinkers saw in it no less than the threat of a return to animality. Cicero compared the organs of the body to children, who may be governed by ordinary methods of discipline, but he acknowledged the presence in their midst of "perverted elements"—the organs of sexuality—that, like disobedient slaves, must be coerced and forced to submit by harsher methods and more stringent rules *(De Republica* 3, 27, 37). Sallust's formulation (in *Catilinae,* chap. 1) was: "our soul directs, our body serves. The one we have in common with the gods, the other with the beasts." Christian theologians later recognized that reason has limitations and that there is danger of incurring arrogance by trusting excessively to its powers. Nevertheless, incurable reasoners that they were, they continued to maintain that reason and virtue were indissolubly linked: To weaken the one was to undermine the other. "The mean of virtue," wrote Saint Thomas Aquinas, "depends not on quantity, but on conformity to right reason." Therefore, the erotic, or as theologians put it, "venereal concupiscence," is to be feared above all because it produces a state of mind that is not subject to the command and moderation of the reasoning faculty.[1]

As to the rebelliousness of man's generational parts (Cicero's "disobedient slaves"), Christian theologians of past eras linked it with the original sin. Adam dared to rebel against God, and in punishment of this *first offense* our body was made to constantly rebel against ourselves. We read in Saint Augustine's *City of God* (book 13, chap. 13) that immediately after the first human beings disobeyed God's instructions, the human soul "rejoiced in its own freedom to act perversely . . . and so it was deprived of the obedient service which its body had at first rendered. . . . This then was the time when the flesh began 'to lust in opposition to the spirit' (Gal. 5:17), which is the conflict that attends us from our birth." Confronted by this depressing interpretation, it is not surprising that the common man should have sometimes disclaimed all responsibility for his sexual transgressions. In a droll anecdote recounted by Tallemant des Réaux, an intemperate Italian gentleman listens with a contrite air, often assenting by nods of his head, to the admonitions of a priest who recommends him continence. The priest paints to the sinner the torments that await him in hell in payment for his intemperate life. At length, the impatient listener interrupts the speech: "Yes, Father, I agree with everything you say . . . " And, after a pause, pointing to his genitals with an expressive Italian gesture of utter frustration, he adds: "*Ma parlate a quèsta bèstia!*" (But now you talk to this beast!)

Medieval moralists were not so sanguine. Their rigid codes decreed undying war to the erotic passion. The desire for pleasure is connatural to us, "especially the pleasures of touch," as Saint Thomas puts it in the *Summa* (question 151, article 2), through which our pitiful species is perpetuated. But the first inward movement of the soul can be modified by temperance. This is crucial: Only those yielding to the first onslaught of lust will be subject to its further spoliations. The virtuous man, like the chaste woman, knows that it is best to nip lust in the bud, lest it grow stubborn and unmanageable, like a spoiled child to whom indulgence of its whims is habitually permitted. Prompted by these thoughts, medieval Christian theologians attempted the systematic repression of man's deepest, most formidable natural drive.

To the early Christian fathers, virginity was the supreme good. "Happy those who still have the power of choosing the better way [glorious virginity], and have not debarred themselves from it by engagements in the secular life," wrote Saint Gregory of Nyssa,[2] regretting that he could not partake of this exalted spiritual pleasure, since he was already married. And in the next few lines he tells us that to yearn for virginity while already being married makes him like a pasturing beast that cannot feed on the inviting grass, or like one who thirsts and cannot drink, or like the victim of other tortures that his rhetorical talent effectively summons. Jerome,[3] in the most famous of his epistles (number 22, to Lady Eustochium), which he wrote in the solitude of his craggy desert, amid scorpions and wild beasts, releases a sweeping condemnation of human sexuality. He reminds the reader that Job, upright before God, said of the devil that "his strength is in the loins, and his force is in the navel" (Job 40:16, speaking of Behemoth). Now, to Jerome (I wonder what psychiatrists would say of him today) this passage of Scripture could only be interpreted as referring to the organs of reproduction, so named for decency's sake. More specifically, we should read: "In his assaults on men, the devil's strength is in the loins; in his assaults on women, his force is in the navel." Accordingly, the good Christian would do well to follow the advice that God gives to Job: "Gird up your loins now, like a man" (Job 38:3). For only so girded can the just confront the temptations of the world.

The sin of fornication is the major peril to be avoided. A Christian marriage may help to counteract this danger, but it is an inferior remedy. Compared to glorious virginity, marriage is a degraded state—"better than to burn," in the famous saying that Saint Paul addressed to the Corinthians, which is really no great recommendation—and, in any case, one incompatible with the highest rewards of religion. The only reason Jerome could find to praise marriage is that it produces virgins *(Laudo nuptias, laudo conjugium, sed quia mihi virgines generant.* Ep. 22). His proposal was "with the axe of virginity to cut down the wood of marriage." It is thus not surprising to hear him dispensing advice to married couples that is the exact opposite of that propounded by contemporary counselors and authors of marriage manuals. Wrote the author of the Vulgate: *Sapiens vir judicio debet amare conjugem, non affectu* (The wise man loves his wife with good judgment, not with feeling). In other words, the married man who cares for the salvation of his soul must guard himself against the role of lover and remain a husband from head to toe.

This uncompromisingly negative view of the erotic must have caused no small amount of suffering. It held in disesteem even the lawful union of the sexes. "If we abstain from intercourse we give honor to our wives; if we do not abstain, it is clear that insult is the opposite of honor." Such was the statement of Jerome in his book *Against Jovinianus* (book 1, 7). Thus, many among the faithful opted to desert the nuptial bed as a way to earn the plaudits of their more zealous brethren. Spouses, of course, could differ among themselves on the intent of domestic life, and disparity of opinion embittered their lives. Saint Abraham was highly praised for having run away from his wife on the night of his wedding. Saint Melania was eulogized for having persuaded her husband to abstain from all intimate contact with her. And after this extreme asceticism had ceased to be held as model for general emulation, its effects continued to be felt for a long time. Couples continued to abstain from sexual activity on the wedding night, as a mark of respect for the sacrament. If by accident they had indulged during religious festivities, processions, or the day of taking the host, they were grievously tortured by a sense of guilt. Pious couples in medieval France could purchase a unique garment known as *chemise cagoule*. This was a feminine sleeping gown of coarse cloth that covered the entire body, so as to limit the opportunities for lustful temptation. It was provided with a small, critically placed orifice, through which the absolute minimum of bodily contact necessary for procreation—and procreation only—could still take place. Although the matter has not been researched by historians, I would wager that the *chemise cagoule* qualifies for the least popular garment ever invented in the history of costume, and the only one that has ever been excepted from the law of cyclically repeated popularity in the history of fashion.

Less well authenticated or semilegendary, a number of other stories exist that give us the temper of those times. During the Diocletian persecution a young Christian was apprehended. Cruel Roman officers wished to see the young man faltering in his faith. Instead of torturing him on the rack, they tied him with silk ribands to a tree, then had a beautiful courtesan try to seduce him while they gave themselves a voyeuristic treat. When the girl appeared dressed for the occasion, the young man closed his eyes to shut off the sensual image but could not close his ears, through which the meretricious temptress slipped suggestive words and lubricious endearments. He could avert his face but not plug his nose to stop the unctuous aroma from invading him. Neither could he, despite his fervorous prayers, anesthetize his bodily surface, on critical parts of which the courtesan endeavored to play all sorts of underhanded tricks. When he felt his fortitude leaving him and his body responding with the predictable localized hyperemia, the young man rabidly bit his tongue and spat the severed tissue, along with spurts of blood, into the woman's face. And the chronicler's rhetoric ends by soaring on the wings of the martyr's inspiring example; with sonorous Latinate periods he tells us that by this shocking expedient the young man succeeded in preserving his glorious virginity, for the defense of which blood, pain, mutilation, and a permanent speech impediment should be accounted as nothing.[4]

In those early Christian times the very sight of woman was insufferable to the pious, let alone the spectacle of feminine wantonness and lechery on the prowl. Saint Prior became a monk and refused to see any woman for thirty years. After this time, his sister implored to be admitted to his presence, for she felt ill and wished to see her brother for the last time. At length he yielded, after arduous persuasion by an interceding abbot. He kept his eyes shut during the whole interview. Another monk shared this aversion and dread of womankind. He was forced to take a trip in the company of his aging mother. He refused to cast his eyes upon her for the whole duration of the trip. They came up to a stream, and as the only bridge had been damaged, it became necessary for the monk to carry his mother on his shoulders. He began carefully wrapping his hands with cloth. The elderly woman asked her son the reason for this unusual preparation. He replied: "The body of woman is like fire, and, were I unlucky enough to touch you, sinful remembrances of femininity might enter into my soul" (*Quia corpus mulieris ignis est, et ex eo ipso quo te contingebat, veniebat mihi commemoratio aliarum feminarum in animo*).

Folly is, without the slightest doubt, universal. But this peculiar variant seems to have been specifically Christian. Among the Jews, the rabbis were expected to be generally chaste, but rabbinic literature never eulogized virginity and monasticism.[5] Scholars have remarked that Halachic discussions on sexual life often reveal a disturbing, unhealthy obsession, attributable perhaps to the stiflingly repressive social conditions that prevailed; but nowhere are virginity and chastity eulogized with the passionate accent of the Christian fathers, who identified these virtues as supreme blessings. It is also true that there were Christian attempts to tone down the early antierotic excess, but they seem halfhearted in comparison with the emphatic condemnation that preceded them. Thus, Saint Thomas was ready to grant that not all venereal acts are sinful: When directed according to reason, there is no opposition to virtue. In the *Summa Theologica* (Part II-II, questions 153 and 154) he sets forth, with the perspicuous propositions of a genial schoolman, the following argument: All reasoning powers are suspended in venereal pleasure, but so they are in sleep, and it cannot be deemed contrary to virtue to set oneself to sleep. But Aquinas's persuasion pales by contrast with Jerome's fiery oratory. Not content with saying that lust is sinful because it leaves the mind in a state incompatible with the act of understanding, the anchorite assures us that lust could render the hearts of the prophets at least momentarily insensitive to the spirit of prophecy. And who would deny the sinful nature of a mental state that deafens the chosen to the word of God?

Opposed to the denigration of sex by Western mysticism, we find its exaltation in mystical-philosophical systems of the Orient.[6] Sexual pleasure was not regarded as a fall or an error but as an experience fit to lead man to self-realization. All invention, all imagination, and all that is worthy in human life may be traced to a desire for pleasure. "He who desires nothing achieves nothing." Manu taught that all that men have created may be reducible to a search for pleasure. And whereas the various organs and bodily senses may be the source of pleasure, the sages maintained the ancient teaching, consigned in the Mahabharata, that every pleasure is necessarily, in some way, erotic. (Curious to note, thousands of years later Freud and his followers heartily concurred with this interpretation.) The Indian sages, therefore, not only abstained from disparaging the erotic experience, but also unambiguously endorsed the notion of its superiority: "The best thing in the seed is the oil, not the residues. The cream is what is best in the milk: flowers and fruits are what is best in the forest. Likewise, pleasure is more important than riches, or virtue."

For oriental mystics, the ultimate goal of life is to achieve a transcendental knowledge. The body, seen as an obstacle to this end in the West, was seen as the instrument, or the means to achieve this goal in the East. Eroticism was the image of the union of the individual being with the universal Being, or Atman, the Spirit of Life. Extreme physical pleasure was like a reflection (and we are reminded of Plato and his world of archetypes) of the perfect happiness. Hence the need for methodical organization in the search for pleasure. The body must be schooled in the ways that intensify and prolong the pleasures of the senses. Hence the writing of erotic treatises: Their aim was not frivolity or titillation, but the earnest preparation of the initiates for a transcending experience that was to carry them beyond the confines of their individual existence. Nevertheless, this purposeful exacerbation of the erotic could not be boundless: The flesh is weak. As Western mystics had to temper their repudiation of sexuality, so did the Eastern faction have to restrain its glorification. Moderation was advised, but only as the necessary condition imposed by the limitations of the body. And their advice was couched in the naturalistic allegories ever dear to mystics East and West: "Oil poured drop by drop into the fire revives the flames, but poured in large gushes smothers them; fields forced to produce too much become infertile: the seed sown in excess fails to grow and is destroyed; likewise, those who give themselves immoderately to pleasure remove themselves from pleasure."

It must not be supposed that the extreme views on the erotic were restricted to the feverish minds of mystics, high-strung with fasts, mortifications, and visions. All who have reflected on the erotic have done so with strong emotions. Lucretius was bothered by the apparent futility in the frantic strivings of sexual passion. In *The Nature of Things,* he compares the couples engaged in the frenzied transports of passion to people who thirst in a stream, and who instead of water are given a semblance or an "idol" of water, and continue to thirst in the middle of the stream. Feverishly do they gaze into each other's eyes. Nervously do they pass their hands in hurried caresses, "as if in the surfeit of their passion they hesitated on what to touch first." Wherefore all the fitful tremors, jactitation, and spasm? For all their enraptured glances, they will fail to see into each other's soul, and for all their anxious caressing, nothing of the skin of one will rub off and pass into the other. Lovers are convinced that they live an extraordinary experience, one that reveals to them somehow the arcane mysteries of the universe. But when the moment comes for them to confirm and validate this momentous experience, how are they to do it? What is the means of expression most commonly employed to pact the magnificent covenant? The body language of sensuality! The stereotyped, atavistic, and mechanical workings of the instincts, and the primeval, spastic responses of the body. Thus, when they say that their love has been "consummated," we are to understand the word *consummation* not in its sense of "bringing to perfection," but as denoting alternating cycles of desire and satiety. Consummation expressed through consumption! This is the paradox that will forever grieve the sensitive and the idealist.

The young speaker in Kierkegaard's "Banquet" is among those who suffer from the paradox.[7] He is deeply puzzled by the "strange gesticulations" and the "mystic tokens" that are proper to erotic love. If two loving souls have found each other and assure one another that they will love one another for all eternity, says the young idealist, this should be quite enough. If one tells the other that this is so, the matter ought to be settled and final. Surely, for people genuinely in love, their saying so should be the most perfect and definitive form of assurance. But, instead, the proof that is demanded, the language that passes for the most valid expression of the covenant, is kisses, embraces, or various forms of bodily contact. "I ask any thinker whether such thing as that has ever entered his mind," rhetorically says the young speaker. "The loftiest psychic experience finds its expression in the extremest contrary, and the sensuous is supposed to indicate the loftiest psychic feeling."

Spiritual, romantic lovers groan under this incongruity. The spirit would soar, but the flesh stays low. Too low. It can scarce be denied that beneath the most exalted symbols of the erotic lie obscure impulses redolent of base animality. Such is our condition, and sooner or later even the spiritual must come to grips with the displeasing fact. The kiss, for instance, on whose symbolism poets and mystics have spent torrents of ink, may hide, at bottom, a trace of anthropophagy. The sinister reminiscences have been all but expunged by centuries of civilization, but in earlier historical periods the frightening meaning may have been more obvious: Egyptologists point out that the same word that was used in ancient Egypt to signify the act of kissing also meant "to eat." Scholarly opinion on the subject, however, has not been inalterable. Prudish times, not surprisingly, produced straitlaced theories. Anthropologists of the Victorian era offered tame interpretations of this most widespread of erotic practices. A French scholar reported that erotic kissing as performed in Europe was entirely unknown in the Far East, and that the Chinese recoiled in horror from the practice of mouth-to-mouth kissing, as from a hideous cannibalistic act. To believe his report, the Chinese favored a different method, described as follows: "The nose is pressed on the cheek, a nasal inspiration follows during which the eyelids are lowered; lastly, there is a smacking of the lips." And the scientist adds with the characteristic pedantry of the professional: "These three phases are clearly distinguished."[8]

Erotic kissing was, therefore, a sort of perversion accruing from our civilization. It was neither universal nor endowed of fixed characteristics. Moreover, respectable Victorian scholars strived to demonstrate that no ideas of biting or anthropophagy could possibly exist in this highly symbolic act, since gustatory elements play no part in kissing. To quote Ernest Crawley in his once popular treatise of anthropology, *The Mystic Rose:* "The kiss, therefore, is not to be referred to the bite, or even to gustation, much less to mastication, suction, or olfactory processes. The primary movement of the lips is simply transferred to a metaphorical use, so to say, and their sensitiveness is applied to a secondary object, whose stimulus is not hunger, but the analogous emotions of love, affection, and veneration."[9] In sum, up to the beginning of the century it was neither tasteful nor scientifically creditable to draw analogies between kissing and eating or biting. Clearly, the romantic faction, to the rejoicement of its disembodied, ethereal, and idealistic membership, had won the upper hand.

Lovers, however, rarely guide their effusions by the prevailing concepts of anthropology. There is evidence that lovers have been very much aware of strong elements of "orality" in kissing, and not ignorant of its gustatory qualities. It suffices to recall the statements of the Shulamite in the Song of Songs (4:11) to be persuaded that *she* was no stranger to the gustatory elements in passionate kisses: "Thy lips drip as the honeycomb, my spouse / Honey and milk are under thy tongue." A Babylonian erotico-religious hymn to the goddess Ishtar,[10] about 1500 years before the birth of Christ, alludes to the sweetness of her lips and to the life-giving properties of her mouth, thus making it likely that the Shulamite's observations on the nontactile delights of lip contact were already old stuff in biblical times. Nor is it true that everyone shared the priggish interpretations of Victorian anthropologists. Contemporary with their researches, Swinburne, decadent poet, was writing these lines:

> By the ravenous teeth that have smitten,
> Through the kisses that blossom and bud,
> By the lips intertwisted and bitten,
> Till the foam has a savor of blood.[11]

There is a charming set piece that Jules Janin wrote in 1826, alluding to the sapid qualities of an erotic kiss, and which I have long believed to represent a sort of allegory of men's views on the erotic, in a broad sense. Janin describes a lively discussion among literary *dilettanti* in a salon. One of them has read the expression "an acrid kiss" in the celebrated novel of Jean Jacques Rousseau, *La Nouvelle Heloïse*. He is intrigued and presents this question for debate to the learned assembly: What could have been the meaning of this utterance, "an acrid kiss," by the putative father of the romantic movement? As it is a problem of no small import to the group, each of its members is eager to discuss it. "Acrid kiss," exclaims a dashing young officer, "is obviously a burning, pungent kiss, the kind that burns, like fire, and stays on our lips indelibly." And while formulating his opinion, the young man sends sidelong glances full of suggestive intelligence to a young lady of the company, who, pretexting to wipe off her mouth, approached a hand-kerchief to her lips, and kept it there for the rest of the soiree.

Next, a middle-aged man rises to voice his opinion. He is the kind in whom, by Janin's appraisal, a not negligible wit is overpowered by robust exuberance. "Acrid kiss," he says, is one that produces the strange sensation of biting an unripe fruit. It is a mixture of pleasant and unpleasant sensations: One desires it one minute and loathes it the next. And the discussant illustrates with an autobiographical detail: "At least that is the effect that produced in me the sole kiss that I ever stole. I still don't know whether the better part of its acridity was enjoyable or disagreeable." But, at this point of the speech so many beautiful mouths in the group tensed, grimaced, and puckered that the speaker was utterly confounded. For, writes Janin, none but the most dogmatic philosopher would have dared to maintain, in the presence of so much oral perfection congregated there, "that feminine mouths and green apples are equivalent."

The turn comes next to a man of the frock who happened to be there. Eyes downcast, voice properly modulated, and demeanor contrite, he starts by apologizing for daring to enter into a debate on matters so distinctly profane and alien to his avocation. Nonetheless, he musters the courage to voice his opinion: "An acrid kiss means the kiss of the unholy, or else of the unshaved." And upon finishing this unsophisticated formulation, so many *boo*s and *bah*s were heard and so many gestures of frank reproof were seen that the would-be oscular expert was repulsed back to his seat and to his theological field, with strong adjurations never to try another sally.

The matter is left undecided. The disputants disband and return to their normal activities. The next day, one of them recounts the savory debate at the office. A band of lively co-workers surrounds him, arguments and counterarguments are exchanged, and the lively debate seems about to restart. At this point, a little man, a petty bureaucrat whom no one ever seems to notice, rises from his chair muttering impatient words at the raucus. The merry assembly, just for laughs, asks his opinion, curious to see what this vulgar and unimaginative fellow, who never reads more than the entertainment section of the newspapers, will have to say about the controversial Rousseauism in question. With pretentious air, after clearing his throat, the man pronounces: "Acrid kiss? Why, it is clear that the writer wished to say that the woman had bad breath."

Janin's exclamations, I have long felt, are applicable to the history of ideas on human eroticism: "O, Rousseau!, O, philosophers! Such is the fate of all the debates of the human spirit. A question is first raised by an original mind. It is next bandied around and bounced by all sorts of wits, and at last a despicable churl comes to settle it forever!"[12]

The views on the erotic have run the full cycle described by

Janin. Idealists repeated for a long time that human eroticism was but one aspect of man's supremely exalted condition: a source of inspiration; the origin of great accomplishments and heroic deeds; adamantine palace where human beings sought refuge while the storm raged outside. Their opponents differed radically: Eroticism was a throwback, a regression to a debased animal condition, a source of irrationality to be avoided at all costs. To the ones, erotic love was the beneficent creative impulse of life, the divine afflatus that impels human beings to reproduce; to the others, it was quite the opposite: Beneath the erotic experience they could descry dark instincts of violence and destruction. In the desire to "fuse" with the beloved, some saw the ultimate manifestation of generosity and self-abnegation of which human beings are capable. Others remarked that a desire for fusion, however metaphoric, implies a wish to efface the boundaries of the individual being, and is, therefore, a death wish. The kiss was to some a symbolic act so powerful, so lofty and spiritual, that none other could better suit the parables in the Gospels. Christ himself resorted to it, in order to impress upon mankind the idea of universal love; Judas, too, to signify treason. But materialists remained unconvinced. The kiss was to them cannibalistic atavism. The most rapturous kiss, they felt, is never far away from the bite of carnivorous animals in heat.

The closing stage in Janin's cycle is imminent. The erotic has ceased to be a sin, or a form of mystical exaltation, or even a passion. It is about to be received as merely a physiological state. Janin's philistine-bureaucrat lives on, and his voice sounds strong. Erotic desire, he says, is wholly comparable to hunger or thirst, *and that is all there is to it*. Passionate behavior is entirely explained as a biochemical disturbance. Love itself is pathology, a sort of recurrent mania. A spate of books, articles, and monographs on orthomolecular psychiatry provides the scientific background for this opinion, which thereby merits today the status of a theory. The philistine party may thus affirm, in proper scientific terminology, that passion is a case of cerebral short circuit or an example of endocrine imbalance. In any event, it is a temporary physiologic breakdown, perfectly amenable to repair by experts in neurotransmission.

It is noteworthy, however, that one and the same faction has simultaneously maintained conflicting views. The Indian mystics who found it easier to attain inner perfection through voluptuosity than through austerity (erotic union and mystic union being, in their view, different aspects of the same experience) had to qualify their endorsement of sensuality with injunctions of restraint. They elevated voluptuosity to the status of first principle, immanent cause, *raison d'être,* source and substance of all creation, but at the same time averred that voluptuosity itself is not creative. Erotic passion is, as the trite saying goes, "consuming fire," self-consuming energy that needs no descendants, seeks no offspring, and aims not to procreate. Siva and Shakti are creative deities of the Indian pantheon, yet the goal of their union is not procreation, but supreme voluptuosity, or sensuality of transcendental nature. Their sex is described in ancient myths in grandiose, epic terms. Siva is lewd, dark, and mysterious. He roams the forests and dances, naked, ejecting from his phallus—swollen with all the creative potentialities of the future—a stream of semen from which originate planets, stones, metals, and jewels. His mate is Energy (Shakti), whose cosmic force is manifested on earth as the energy that spews out of the top of mountains (and hence her name Parvati, from *parvata,* mountain). Nevertheless, the world, in this cosmology, is not engendered by the union of Siva and Shakti. They each have a son, but each is born independently, not as a result of the union. Supreme eroticism is always barren.

Whatever conclusions be drawn from the discrepant views, certain it is that there is a sunny and a shady side to the erotic. Crass materialists cannot deny the ennobling and spiritual qualities of an experience that, like no other, can bring two separate individualities close to each other. In a world torn by dissension and embittered by rancor, this alone is no small recommendation. Likewise, the spiritual and the idealist also have to accept that the erotic experience has a distressing underside. Whatever ineffable consolations and triumphs they might derive from love's spiritual aspects, they must grant that human sexual love cannot be stripped clean of its sinister primeval roots; that flesh is the stuff of which we are made, and that this is, indeed, a flawed and most unreliable material.

As to the philistine sect, I must say that I agree with its central tenet but disagree with its recommendations. Love *is* pathology (I am now speaking solely of erotic passion, not of the many felicitous arrangements and combinations by which sexual needs, and material and spiritual wants, are reconciled, leading to a happy, durable union). When experienced strictly as passion, love is eminently disquieting. It is unreasonable and plainly dangerous. It is neither useful nor conformable to law. It is not normal. It is entirely alien to the social order and actuated by principles of its own, which have nothing to do with marriage, the stability of our social position, or community of interests of the participants. Since it is absolutely disinterested, it is unconcerned with legal questions, and therefore duty, institutions, social order, progeniture, estate, and the like mean absolutely nothing to it. Clearly, a man professing such persuasions would be indistinguishable from a madman. The philistine faction does well in recommending medical treatment for such an individual. But I would withhold assent on the premise that the same condition that brings some to ruin impels others to greatness.

Recollect the clinical course of a famous madman, who styled himself "Knight of the Rueful Countenance." Pining away for a woman of scarce merit, whom in his lunacy he fancied a noble princess, he withdrew to as inhospitable and lone a spot as he could find in a remote mountain. There, amid bare rocks and thorny bushes, he set about to do penance, as a token of his love and in conformity with the rules of chivalry. He announced that in imitation of his forerunner, the great Beltenebros, he would choose a harsh style of penance. This consisted in knocking his head against the rocks, and after stripping himself of his clothes, except for his shirt, doing capers in the air and somersaults heels over head. In the performance of the latter, "he exposed such parts as, not to see them a second time, his squire wheeled round," leaving his master to continue performing these and other crazy feats. Representatives of the philistine party—as strong then as now—came to fetch him. They were as one in recommending treatment, but the state of medical science was so poor that all they could do was to watch him and keep him under close supervision.

There exist today highly effective therapies for such disorders. There is no reason to doubt that had these been available at the time, their benefit would have been granted to the illustrious patient. Some would have advocated what is known as "aversive electrical stimulation for behavior modification." A good shock every time our man conceived the idea of redressing mischief, and double the dose if the avenging required drawing a sword or leveling a lance. Until recently, there was a good chance that the self-styled knight-errant would have been subjected to psychosurgery of some kind. But perhaps in our day the likelihood is greater that physicians would have opted to remove the barber's basin that the patient took for miraculous helmet, then to place two electrodes against his scalp and pass an electric current of about 0.8 ampere through his brain, a procedure that sends the patient convulsing for about a minute or a minute and a half. It is a drastic remedy, no doubt, but currently much in favor in the most advanced countries: In the province of Ontario alone, some twenty thousand treatments of this kind are yearly administered to patients, each of whom gets, on the average, about ten courses in two weeks.[13]

Our patient, I am convinced, would feel no desire to do capers, somersaults, or head-banging once he had received a full course of our modern treatment. But neither, I am afraid, would he feel the slightest inclination to the toils of knight-errantry. For it seems plain to me that the same kind of inner energy that compels him to capers, somersaults, and head-banging is also the driving force behind the desire to slay monsters, engage giants in singular combat, and free innocent maidens from captivity. And this, in a nutshell, is my argument against the philistine solution. The latter would give us a world without madmen. But it would also be a world without men desirous to be counted among those who, sustained only by the memory of their mistresses, "have done, are doing, and will do the most famous deeds . . . that in this world have been seen, are to be seen, or ever shall be seen."

ON SECRECY IN LOVE

"All passions are deceptive, for they conceal themselves as much as possible from others and from themselves as well. No vice exists which does not pretend to be more or less like some virtue, and which does not profit from this assumed resemblance." So spoke La Bruyère in *The Characters of Theophrastus,* and with his terse statement we feel compelled to agree. All who ever hastily and in calculated stealth passed a crumpled bit of paper containing a culpable message; who ever held a warm, soft hand under a desktop or behind a chair's back while pretending to follow attentively the lesson, exposition, or sermon; who furtively slipped an ardent utterance into unprovided ears, immediately to fake an air of innocence or contrition when the vigilance resumed; all these, I say, will grant that dissembling is not the least of love's adjuncts, and that conspiracy and stratagem are as much interwoven in its fabric as are sighs and swoons. For who is so pure or so wise as never to have needed the simple private codes by which lovers communicate the thoughts that they deem exclusively their own? One flower in a vase by the window means "meet me at the appointed place"; a whole bouquet, "the rendezvous is off." Curtains drawn mean a certain thing; open, an altogether different one. Love is the supreme lexicographer and the foremost nonverbal communicator. With faked coughs, quick rubbing of fingers, pressures with a foot, and glances full of intent, a ponderous treatise might easily be written.

The tradition is a long one. The ancient Indian sutras dispense abundant advice on secrecy to lovers. The celebrated *Kama Sutra,* whose lyrical descriptions of erotic acts have titillated the prurience of readers and sparked the disapprobation of censors for thousands of years, lists dozens of amatory themes of utility to lovers. Not the least of them is the ability to write in code; this important art is recommended to the notice of all who would aspire to passable success in matters erotical. Through the centuries, inventiveness put at the service of the lovers' cause underwent significant refinements; of its moral objectives it is not possible to say that the change was always for the better. Queen Marie Antoinette, awaiting her trial and under the very nose of her stern captors, was able to engage in political conspiracy and in voluminous amorous correspondence with Count Fersen by writing in cipher. The key was later explained by Princess Marie Thérèse de Lamballe in her memoirs and shown to be no example of cryptographic complexity. Lovers, however, will always show themselves equal to the challenge: When pressed by adverse circumstances they will contrive the means of establishing the desired contact in one form or another.

When I was growing up in Mexico City, the prevailing

mores were not especially bountiful to male youths in search of dalliance. In the lower-class district that witnessed the pristine eclosion of my manhood, careful planning was indispensable to thwart the vigilance of violent, obdurate brothers, or the less inflexible zeal of sisters, cousins, and assorted chaperones. Inventiveness, resourcefulness, and those skills that others cultivate through chess-playing or youth-edifying sports it fell to us to promote under the relentless spur of nascent sex. Opportunities had to be sought with unflagging diligence; success was the reward of a strategist's skill. A prime occasion was the daily shopping for victuals for the household, usually entrusted to girls. Milk vendors opened late, and under cover of darkness the nightly sallies achieved transactions more varied than those solely of interest to economists, while a popular rural song instructed the beginner in quaintly vulgar lyrics:

> *Como que chiflo y tú sales,*
> *Como que vas por la leche,*
> *Si no eres tonta ya sabes.*

> I'll whistle, do you come out
> Pretend you go milk-a-shopping
> You are no dunce, you know what I mean.

It is with love as with all of man's affairs: Its cast is foreordained in the arcane designs of fate. The privileged few sense the first tugs of love amid the dazzle and sparkle of luxury; the first embrace in sumptuous surroundings, with ruffling of silk and clinking of jewels; the first touch of hands in view of inspiring, sublime settings. For millions of American youths the shrine that framed the first oblation was the inside of an automobile: The officiating votaries had at least the chance of removing themselves from importunity and of casting hurried ɡlances through a rearview mirror when, by rare exception, their unctional transports did not take away the better part of their circumspection. It was appointed that my lot should be different. As the ancient worshippers of Aphrodite traveled to sacred Cythera, I journeyed to the local dairy. The aroma of the essences of Syria was for me the smell of cream and pasteurized milk, sold by the liter; the priestess of Cyprus, a brune Mestiza of pitch-black braids; and the entrancing, hieratic dance, the strutting of a swarthy maid who balanced pots of skimmed or two percent on rhythmically swaying, opulent hips. Nor shall I ever complain of my luck. Milk is on a par with the perfumes of Arabia. Higher yet: It flowed from the breast of the goddess, to be spread in the sky as the starry road of the empyrean. And if milk never passed for an aphrodisiac, its role as an accessory in erotic undertakings was not wholly neglected, either. Ovid's *Art of Love* contains recipes for the elaboration of invisible inks, by means of which those inclined to engage in extramarital affairs could send messages without fear of being discovered. Fresh milk was one of Ovid's rudimentary technical inventions: when gently rubbed with coal dust, the message written in milk becomes visible.

At that time, some of us complained that barred windows, ubiquitous chaperones, and male relatives with a hypertrophic sense of family honor were anachronistic residua of a past, barbaric era. The fashion was to attribute these repressive measures to what passes for ferociously conservative traditionalism in Spanish culture. Spaniards, in turn, were quick to pass the blame for these social attitudes to their Islamic historical influence. Were they right? It is for professional historians to decide. We, the laymen, form our opinions through quick and easy impressions. We canvass the colorful features of daily life in the ancient Arab world as presented in popular works of history and fiction, and are struck by the richness of its imagery: We see men of opulent hedonism and an inborn taste for convoluted formal design; we see women, the proper match of these men, managing to exert their wiles in spite of face-veiling and harsh confinement.

Nor is it right to assume that a natural sensuality dictated rules of greater permissiveness in such a society, as the unexpurgated translations of numberless erotic tales and poetry of the period might lead one to suspect. True, a paradise populated by courtesans and sensual delights was promised to faithful men in this society, but this was only because heaven was regarded as the place where a highly valued recompense could be bestowed. Earth, however, was the place to earn the award, and chastity was its proper sphere. Hence the Islamic bent to make things difficult for lovers and to place guards, barriers, and frightful penalties in the way of erotic emprise. Add to all this the rule of some fearful despot, a sheikh, caliph, or sultan, as hawklike in his mien as in his style of government, ready to tear with his talons any and all who would be careless enough to elicit his displeasure. The result is a society where commerce between the sexes is anything but free and unimpeded. The ability to perceive a hidden signal, like a Koranic script encoded upon an overweight ornamental decor, is much more than a learned cultural trait: It is an indispensable requirement for survival.

Given this background, it is not surprising that the theme of erotic intrigue should have reached considerable development in Arabic literature. One of its outstanding productions is *The Dove's Neck,* a book written by the poet Ibn Hazm[1] (A.D. 994–1063) during the medieval caliphate of Córdoba. The son of an influential politician, Ibn Hazm passed his childhood in the languid atmosphere of the harems, amid the pampering and kisses of the women, attentive to their chattering and gossip. The women of the seraglio taught him his first Koranic verses, held his hand while it awkwardly squiggled its first written lines, and opened his eyes to the enervating and sumptuous world of sensuality, as once known in the Middle East. This early experience was not lost in the future poet and political activist. In *The Dove's Neck,* we find profuse advice on the keeping of amorous secrets, on spies, calumniators, go-betweens, and all manner of intriguers. In discussing the qualities that are most desirable in confidants, to whom a chapter is devoted, the poet says that they must be men of clear judgment; always available; true friends; capable of sorting out imbroglios; faithful to their pledges; and of constant temperament, lively disposition, and chaste nature. Where to find such a friend, the poet does not say. So many qualities are rarely found together in one person. Thus, the lover in need of relieving his soul of a burden has two choices: either to talk to the air and the rocks in some solitary place or else to resign himself to confide in the uncaring, the disdainful, or the indiscreet. He has, however, another option: The male lover may confide in a woman. Almost *any* woman. Ibn Hazm declares that he knows of no woman who ever maliciously exposed the secret of two lovers, if not from jealousy.

However, one thing is the confidant, mere depositary of our secrets, and another the active accomplice of our deeds, the go-between. Considering the precarious balance of amorous relationships in medieval Córdoba, the office of go-between must have been an extremely delicate one, indeed. A billet-doux could not be sent off with just *anyone*. "The sender's life or death, concealment or shame, rests in his hands, after being in those of Allah, The Most High." The fundamental requirement in go-betweens is inconspicuousness. The best ones are servants whom no one notices due to their young age, their shabby clothes, or the manifest stupidity of their faces. There is, of course, the opposite type: respectable persons who do not arouse suspicion because of their pious background or advanced age. Here, again, this type is most frequently found among women, "especially those who walk with canes [and] carry rosaries," and is particularly abundant in the professions that require contact with people, such as salesgirl, hairdresser, card-reader, weaver, hired mourner, healer, applier of suction cups, and the like. Evidently, *dueñas* and *celestinas,* the proverbial go-betweens of Spanish literature, trace their hoary lineage to this ancient Islamic precursor.

In this world of officious intriguers, clandestine communication, and sly dissimulation, lovers have a major peril to contend with: the spy. Ibn Hazm's concept of spies is a broad one: They are those individuals who through their actions, voluntary or involuntary, contribute to expose the affair that lovers wished to maintain occult. There are three major categories of spies: the importune, the curious, and the authentic. The importune kind comprises those individuals who linger interminably in the places where lovers meet. They do not wish to discover the affair but are no less noxious to its viability. To the lovers, these characters are "heavies": detestable and burdensome in the extreme. In a poetic hyperbole that loses none of its flavor for traveling across ten centuries and immense transcultural chasms, they are branded "heavier than Mounts Saman, Radwa, Lukam, Yabdul, Lebanon, Samman, and Hazn" (mountains of the Arab world frequently used as topics of Islamic poetry). The curious spy, in contrast, is pernicious because of his nimble mind. Having spotted a clue to the love affair, he is piqued to uncover the whole thing. He acts of his own accord and purely out of fondness for detective work.

Curious spies today would count themselves among Agatha Christie's fans, and perhaps among "Baker Street's Irregulars." In Ibn Hazm's time they were recognized as fundamentally injurious to love affairs, in the measure that they felt disposed to follow the promptings of their own curiosity.

Neither of the two previous sorts is as dangerous as the authentic spy, that is, one who is paid to safeguard the chastity of one of the lovers. Woe to the lovers when an authentic spy shows zeal in the discharge of his functions! No greater misfortune can befall those who, in love, are visited by this plague. The only remedy is to spot him and to try to win him over by bribery or whatever means. But there is no set pattern to amorous intrigue with spy participation. This the author of *The Dove's Neck* makes plain with illustrative case reports. A lover may become a spy, and conversely, a spy may become a lover. The complexity of intrigue is further instanced with the following true observation. A spy falls in love with the person spied on. When this becomes known by the first lover (the instigator of the spying), this one becomes a spy who eagerly spies on the first spy.

Our author reserves generous space to indirect verbal communication. A chapter is devoted to insinuation, as by suggestive proverbs or ambiguous phrases, and how these may be cunningly dropped by those who mean to declare their passion (without being understood by unwelcome third parties). Nonverbal communication is amply discussed. Paramount among nonverbal expressions are the signals made with the eyes. Consider the sophisticated examples described in the appropriate chapter. A signal made by the corner of the eye denotes veto to the thing asked for. A languid glance signifies acceptance. If the gaze is sustained, the message is one of pain and sadness. A rapid gaze that quickly slides over us, as it were, indicates joy. To turn the pupils to a given site, then withdraw them abruptly, is a way to call attention to that which is seen. One may threaten by half closing the eyes and supplicate by sending forth a furtive signal from the corners of the eyes. Absolute prohibition is expressed with certain pupillary motions that start from the center of the orbits. Ends Ibn Hazm's exposition of visual expressions: "I have tried to set forth the things that seem easier to describe, although these signs, unseen, can hardly be described. There are many others [such as those made to promise, to repel, to encourage, to thunder against servants, and to warn against spies], but those can only be understood by actually seeing them." Evidently, it was not easy to conduct love affairs in Muslim Spain during the tenth century. I must thank Providence for having spared me such toil. However taxing it was for me to be forced into periodic forays to the milk shop, the labors demanded of me never required this exquisite pupillary control. Nor does it seem likely that, hampered as I was by profound myopia of early onset, I could have achieved any decent progress in this very important department of human activity.

Today, nonverbal communication will simply not do. The abstract concepts that have always been the central theme of the lovers' discourse are best conveyed through the use of language. But here lies another difficulty: Language serves us well only for as long as we move in the trivial world of daily life. Not so in the lofty regions of abstraction. "Pass me the salt" or "my soup is cold" are utterances about whose meaning no one seems to dispute. But no sooner do we quit the consuetudinary than words begin to lose their sharpness. Already in the realm of mathematics, words and sentences are best discarded: Symbols and formulas are used in their stead. The higher we climb upon the abstract, the more we reckon the dictionary a useless encumbrance to the ascent. Reflect, though, that the experience lived by lovers lies higher yet than mathematics. It unfolds atop the most forbidding peaks, since those who climb the extraordinary heights always report dizziness and vertigo. How are lovers to frame this experience in words when the words carry no meaning and cannot be uttered in the rarefied air? How are they to engage in private conversation? Rather, how are they to communicate at all, seeing the lack of a suitable language? Medicine, botany, and aeronautics possess specialized terminologies. Computer engineers, like sailors or marketing experts, may talk to each other in a language that excludes the uninitiated. But love is either deaf-mute or a plagiarist. Its utterances are always borrowed, and the lover must make do with tools on loan.

It has often been remarked that lovers tend to use the language of religious mystics. There are those who retort by saying that mystics use the language of lovers, but I always felt that behind such rejoinders stood a not negligible amount of bad faith. "To worship," "to adore," "to be consumed by," and "to die for" seem expressions more properly directed to an everlasting deity than to the saucy, mortal object of veneration who often poses as recipient. Stendhal pushed effrontery to the point of saying that the statue of Saint Teresa of Avila, by Bernini, was the most sensual sculptoric composition that he had ever seen. In the mystic trance of the saint, whose joints loosen and whose unseen body slumps under a flowing nun's habit, he thought he saw I know not what orgasmic climax. The likes of Stendhal, I am afraid, will always gravitate more toward idolatry than to the gift of grace. But it is true that religious mystics have often spoken in words indistinguishable from those of profane lovers. The two, to believe a respectable school of thought in psychiatry, are closer to each other than habitually surmised. The lover who feels an inexpressible emotion at the sight of objects that he associates with the beloved; who perceives a mysterious "charge" as he runs his fingers through a garment that was once worn by the beloved; who discerns an indefinable new meaning in buildings, trees, and common things, as if the beloved had infused them with a transcendent quality; such a one is no doubt closer to believing in the Catholic dogma of transubstantiation than many a devout zealot after protracted theological indoctrination. All of which underscores the lack of a true lovers' language. At its most exalted, the lovers' discourse is disputed by religious mystics—precisely the faction most bitterly opposed to agree with the lover's intended meaning.

More subdued or less romantic forms of speech are also shared. The lover who declares himself "constant," "loyal," or "seriously committed," uses terms that a political activist might claim as his own. When lovers profess to have undergone the most radical change of their lives, their speech might pass for that of a revolutionist. In the grip of erotic obsession, the lover is convinced of having taken a new identity. Such a man is, in a strict sense, a revolutionist. The married man, like the married woman, swayed by an extramarital love passion may declare all former contractual obligations invalid. Mark the extent of the subversion: It is not enough for him to say that he is no longer accountable to wife, children, or society (since he is no longer himself after the revolutionary experience); still more, he will attack the very grounds on which his obligations were based. He will assert that it is wrong to subordinate love to the clauses of a contract, because love does not depend on one's will. If he is told that his personal feelings must take second place to his obligations to others, he will answer that this is impossible, since he is no longer himself. For the "new man" (is it not a common revolutionary slogan, "to create a new man"?) life is unendurable if it must be lived away from his beloved. All former ties, all preconceptions must be sacrificed—and here, again, is this not the speech of a revolutionist? Perchance we tell him that he is free to love but must conform to the exigencies of society. A wife, perhaps, will plead with him to stay for the sake of appearances. He will then unleash the "hard line" of his new ideology. He will rejoin that we are all hypocrites or philistines who pay lip service to human freedom but condemn a man to despair for the sake of form. The man is clearly a subversive, a seditious doctrinaire, the upholder of a logic that is not like the logic of the rest of us.

Nor can we expect of governments that profess to be revolutionary that they will create a lovers' vocabulary compatible with lovers' needs. Political ideologues, like mystics, distrust erotic love, and with good reason. It is a fundamentally private experience, and an irrational one at that. It can neither fit into a rational doctrinal corpus nor thrive in perfect unison with the public weal. Revolutionists, therefore, have always enforced the keeping of erotic love securely away from the public domain. Now and then we hear of attempts to reconcile love's speech with partisan terminology, but these efforts are always ludicrous. During a period of ideological effervescence, a Moscow radio broadcast in 1952 staged a courtship scene between two young collective farm workers. As the scene progressed, the girl, who drove a tractor, sighed: "How wonderful it is to work on such a beautiful moonlit night, and do one's best to save fuel!" To which romantic exclamation the boy answered: "The night inspires me to overfill my quota by a higher and still higher percentage." And it is said that the simple declaration "I love you" took this gauche appearance for a time among Burmese communists: "I am deeply impressed by your faith in our country's goals, and I wish to wage the Party's struggle together with you."[2]

The lack of an idoneous language turns some lovers into laughable mountebanks. It may also transform the eloquent into babblers. Victor Hugo was more than articulate: He was torrentially grandiloquent. Yet, when in need of a private erotic language, he seems to have lapsed into linguistic inadequacy. He found no better way to dissimulate the erotic entries of his diary than to write them in Spanish. Biographers note that Hugo chased young girls when well into his eighties. Because he feared that his diary could be surreptitiously read by his wife, he described his conquests in telegraphic style, with keywords in Spanish (the verb *acostar,* "to bed," recurs frequently). As if jotting down his knavish tricks in a language structurally similar to his own, at a time when French artists raved about all things Spanish, had been sufficient guarantee that the scabrous passages would not be understood!

Equally disconcerting is the case of Jonathan Swift. The great Dean of St. Patrick ate on second table (i.e., with the servants) at the house of Sir William Temple, and there nurtured a rage in his heart that stirred his genius into bitter fury. Of him, Orerry wrote: "He had a natural severity of face, which even his smiles could scarce soften, or his utmost gaiety render placid and serene; but when that sternness of visage was increased by rage, it is scarce possible to imagine looks or features that carried in them more terror and austerity." Picture this fearful wit tearing down men in office, lashing furiously in his writings at any and all that awaken his wrath. And see him, next, penning down childish endearments and "baby talk" to the woman he loved, Esther Johnson ("Stella"). In his correspondence to Stella, *dood mollow* stands for "good morrow," *rove* for "love," and so on.

Assuredly, Swift was plunged, as Thackeray wrote, "into woeful pitfalls and quagmires of amorous perplexity." But Swift is not an isolated case. "Baby talk" is often used by lovers. It may be simply a way to keep outsiders uninformed of the exchange, but it is not clear why the private language should be a regressive one. Psychiatrists have not fully explained the use of infantine gabble in erotic affairs. Writers of farce have abundantly exploited the figure of the old and gouty lecher who addresses saccharine blandishments to a young woman. Is he trying to turn back the clock, but so eagerly that he "overcompensates," as some have thought? If the young woman lends herself to the game and replies in kind, she may do so out of charitableness: She admits into her maternal bosom a superannuated lover and a symbolic child. Scholarly opinion on Swift's babbling is not so complacent. It has been suggested that his childish expressions may have been a premonition of his cerebral disintegration. Swift, as is well known, suffered from a mysterious degenerative disease of the brain. He was officially declared insane in 1742, and guardians were appointed to him by the Court of Chancery. Wrote Thackeray: "An immense genius: an awful downfall and ruin . . . Thinking of him is like thinking of an empire falling. We have other great names to mention—none, I think, however, so great or so gloomy."

Our era brought one solution to the problem of clandestine amorous communication. Magazines and newspapers, since the early nineteenth century, became the unwitting adjuncts of Cupid. This one shot his arrows through the personal ads section of the newspapers. Donald McCormick, in his charming, slim book,[3] tells us that in England the tradition goes back to 1800, when the *Times* published its "agony column"— so called from its frequent use by anguished persons who pleaded with missing relatives to come forward—which became the vehicle for secretive love communications. Singular items (for example: "xsihnjtkdkghj ldkdjllg" and so on) started appearing that could not be said to offend public morals or raise suspicion in vigilant spies. The jealous wariness of the latter never extended to banning from the household so innocent an item as an issue of a regular newspaper. And yet the contrivance was not foolproof. Intrigued by these cryptic messages, two brainy English gentlemen, Charles Wheatstone and Lyon Playfair, set about to decipher them. Playfair was later made a baron, president of the British Association for the Advancement of Science, and for a time Deputy Speaker of the House of Commons.

Imagine the two respectable, Victorian English gentlemen concerting to crack the code of the mysterious daily messages. As others take to solving crossword puzzles or collecting stamps, these two look forward to solving the riddle of the recurring enigmas printed in the *Times*. Their hobby grows into an all-consuming obsession. They take notes; they consult works on code decipherment; they turn the messages about in their heads, ceaselessly, sometimes even in their sleep. At last the solution is gleaned: The writer had inverted the spelling, alternated meaningful and meaningless letters, and purposefully neglected punctuation. No matter: All his cunning was undone by two minds pitted against his, and steadfast in their purpose.

What joy, discovery! Wheatstone and Playfair must have known the thrills of Archimedes unraveling the principles of mechanics or Newton discovering the law of gravity. Their ineffable delights are best likened to those of Champollion piecing together the great puzzle of the Rosetta stone. Yet the hieroglyphics that Champollion read spoke of esoteric concepts of transmigration, whereas the various scripts that Playfair and Wheatstone deciphered week after week stood for the stirring accent of human passion, alive and palpitating. And whereas the scholars of the past, gazing into the ruins of disappeared civilizations, could only conjecture about the validity of their conclusions, Playfair and Wheatstone could test the truth in theirs with all the rigor of experimental science.

Their confirmatory tests had all the respectability of the scientific method. One of the cryptologists validated a hypothesis by no less than predicting a future observation. He had been following the coded amorous correspondence of two lovebirds whose effusions had gradually mounted in temperature, unaware that somewhere in the same city a bespectacled, middle-aged man made it a point of pride to understand their messages after translating the apparently impenetrable hocus-pocus. At last the lovers agreed to meet in an out-of-the-way place. The woman, who obviously had reasons to fear being discovered, was to appear veiled but attired in such a way as to be recognized from a distance without any need to uncover her face. When the two lovers met, quickly to slink into a room at an inn, little did they suspect that one of the customers of the place was actually a cryptologist privy to their secret, and who watched them with the glowing satisfaction of the scientist who sees his hypothesis confirmed. In fact, the two English gentlemen had come upon the felicitous combination that was privately envied by many a Victorian man: They could snoop into the private lives of people—even, on occasion, indulge in a little voyeurism—and do all this under the guise of practicing an arduous intellectual exercise. It seems that Playfair and Wheatstone became consummate cryptologists with this practice. They developed their own secret writing-code, so undecipherable that they proposed it to the Foreign Office, suggesting that it could be used in covert international operations promoted by the British secret service. McCormick says that their proposal was turned down when the under secretary objected that it was "too complicated."

It is very unlikely that the deciphering skills of these two gentlemen would find much application in today's newspapers. A sexually permissive social climate and the proliferation of veritable subcultures in the midst of what used to be culturally homogeneous social classes have produced a corresponding increase in lexicons. Thus, one finds today in the classified ads section of newspapers and magazines not the coded messages that translate into free-flowing conventional English prose, but overt messages that can only be understood by the initiates, i.e., the members of the appropriate subculture. As an example, I transcribe the paid notes that were published in the March 28, 1986 issue of the *Reader,* a Chicago weekly magazine distributed by the downtown merchants of this city:

"PEE WEE: Tortillas at the Alamo sounds lovely. Can the Jelly Donuts come along if they bring their hibachi? Just call me Miz Bungle. Miss Yvonne."

A peculiar note was couched in irreverent religious imagery:

"MARY MAGDALENE—SORRY I haven't written, but the old stigmata has been acting up again. Padre Pio."

In the April 25 issue I find this peculiar message:

"JOE DUST, rhythmatic thumposaurus, post acidic stelcholas, light and rok."

Secrecy, stealthiness, and conspiracy: love has softly trodden this triple path even when its ends were legitimate. What may be obtained by petition is often got by obreption; what may be said clearly is frequently couched in terms that only the lovers understand. When an official engagement, backed by the community's sanction, is not sufficient to deter the affianced from chronic secrecy and underhandedness, it may well be imagined that an illicit affair brings out the best and most Machiavellian of their conspiratorial talents. One example among millions of possible ones should suffice. Tradition has it that a French lady, Madame de la Popelinière, became entangled in an amorous intrigue with a French aristocrat about the year 1744. The man was the Duke of Richelieu, Marshal of France, and the place of the assignations was his sumptuous mansion. To the lovers' dismay, this house was located on the street of Clichy, not too far away from the conjugal domicile of the disloyal woman. It became necessary for the adulterous couple to resort to disguises, watchmen, passwords, and the many other ruses that have been styled in those cases ever since the invention of monogamy. And as has also been the usual occurrence, their subterfuges had limited effectiveness, and their trickery went unsuspected only for a short time.

The husband did not look upon these matters with philosophical resignation. Seeing himself the target of sassy and unfeeling innuendo, he became enraged. However, he did not dare to oppose his powerful rival. In consequence, he resorted to still another practice as old as the institution of marriage: wife battering. By an official deposition at the Châtelet, it became a matter of historical record that Madame de la Popelinière complained, on the morning of April 24, 1746, that she had been physically mistreated by her husband the night before. She showed to the appropriate official the bruises that kicks by her husband had left on her arms and legs. The bureaucrat noted that she had called a physician to take care of her injuries, and that the treatment had consisted of two bleeds (one would have sufficed, we are led to understand, had the injuries been less serious). When the duke heard of this incident and realized the magnitude of the potential danger, he resolved to act in such a way as to decrease the chances for the recurrence of violence—without renouncing the lady's favors. In order to secure this end, he devised a plan that was to produce one of the great technological achievements of the eighteenth century, although one of the least known. It may be referred to as "the revolving hearth," and the circumstances of its creation will be described presently.

The duke realized that his mistress's bedroom, on the second floor of her residence, was provided with a large fireplace against the wall adjoining the next house. Money was no obstacle to our man. He began by buying the adjoining house. Next, he placed a woman of his confidence in the capacity of concierge. The next step of the plan was carried out with meticulous attention to details. Desnoyers, a master craftsman, and a crew of workers were hired to carry out a construction job that required speed and exquisite precision. Upon the promise of a very generous remuneration, the workers were persuaded to come to the construction site with banded eyes and were transported in a carriage that deliberately took long detours and followed a circuitous route. Once inside the duke's newly acquired building, the bandage was removed, and they were informed of the nature of the job. They were to cut a hole in the wall that would establish a communication with the adjacent room, that is, the bedroom of the duke's mistress, and then to dissimulate the opening as best they could. The duke knew that the neighbors, Monsieur and Madame de la

Popelinière, were away for one week. Nevertheless, he offered the workers fifty *louis* if the assignment was completed in one night. With cries of joyous anticipation at so bountiful a reward, the crew set to work. They fashioned a trapdoor that was a marvel of workmanship: Not only were the pieces reassembled with technical perfection, so that the junctions were virtually invisible, but they also added an ingenious hinged mechanism by which the replaced panels opened and closed without difficulty once a button was pressed. Seen from the lady's bedroom, the secret passage opened into a recessed brick fireplace whose soot-covered, shaded surface could easily have concealed any marks of the workers' activity, had there been any. From the duke's room the communication was equally inconspicuous; nevertheless, he took the precaution of covering the area with a large mirror. Desnoyers and his assistants were removed from the premises with as many secrecy measures as had been used to bring them in, so that none could tell the location of the house in which their masterpiece had been executed.

In the ensuing months, Madame de la Popelinière rarely ventured out of her house. Her husband attributed this voluntary seclusion to a newly kindled acceptance of the rules of domestic life; and no doubt, in his blindness, he thought the blows he had given her were instrumental in reinforcing obedience to the commands of conventional morality. The truth was that the lovers were now at liberty to profit from the husband's absences with greater frequency than before. Through a dutiful sentry watch, unfailingly performed by the duke's concierge, the lovers were adequately forewarned when danger was approaching. The duke could then exit from Madame de la Popelinière's bedroom as expeditiously as he had entered across the concealed passageway. These complicated shenanigans were not without risk. On one occasion the duke hit the wall with a series of loud blows, the preconvened signal that he wished to visit his mistress if the coast was clear, precisely at the time that Monsieur de la Popelinière had come into his wife's bedroom. The wife remained calm. She faked irritation at the "constant noise" with which their neighbors disturbed her peace, grabbed the fire tongs from the fireplace, and struck the wall several times, as if to let the neighbors know of her displeasure. This was, of course, the coded message signifying to her lover that there was immediate danger. The lover made no more noise, and the husband, utterly reassured of the insignificance of the incident, thought no more of impertinent neighbors tapping on the wall at odd hours.

These goings-on could not have been maintained indefinitely. A maid became suspicious at the insistence with which the lady of the house locked herself up inside her bedroom, always turning the key, when there seemed to be no need for this precaution. She spied, and distinctly heard a masculine voice in her lady's bedroom. She saw the potential for material profit and attempted blackmail, whereupon she was dismissed from the household. She was spiteful and denounced the wrongdoings in a letter to the outraged husband. This one conducted a meticulous search in his wife's bedroom without finding a trace of the trapdoor. On the morning of November 28, 1748, husband and wife had to attend a troop review on the plains of Sablons, near Chaillot, having been summoned thereto by Marshal de Saxe. La Popelinière, under the pretext of a sudden malaise, left his wife in the carriage of the mighty and influential marshal, and no sooner had it started off on its way to Sablons than he returned home accompanied by two of his friends, Vaucanson and the lawyer Savot. With their help, he wished to conduct a new investigation, this time leaving no square centimeter of his wife's bedroom unexamined.

They had palpated the entire room, tile by tile, board by board, when the lawyer friend remarked that the fireplace showed no signs of recent use in spite of the rigors of the season. On all fours, he examined the surface of the fireplace and knocked on it forcefully with his cane. A hollow sound encouraged him to pursue the investigation, until at last he discovered the hidden trapdoor. At that time he exclaimed:

"Ah! Monsieur, what an admirable workmanship! Why, there is here a movable plank, but the hinge is utterly hidden, and so delicately fashioned!"

"Are you sure it opens?" asked the betrayed husband, turning pale.

"Of course it opens. Come and admire this magnificent piece of craftsmanship."

"Admire? Pray, monsieur, spare me your ironies. We did not come here to admire."

"I am terribly sorry. It is just that these days one no longer sees workers who take pride in what they do. I used to know some that were true artists. Whoever made this beautiful door, let me tell you . . . "

"Leave your beautiful door alone. Let's unhinge it," answered La Popelinière abruptly, and the three men went on to expose the whole deceitful trickery.

Violence was averted when the unfaithful wife returned, thanks to the prudent intercession of la Popelinière's obliging friends. Nonetheless, he refused to admit her into the conjugal domicile and stood deaf to her supplications. The gossip-prone social circle in which the couple had moved relished the scandal. They took to this near-tragedy with the proverbial playfulness and lightness of heart of the *ancien régime*'s upper class.

Paris raved over a new style of fashion called *à la Popelinière,* which included coiffures, tobacco boxes, fans, dresses, and jewelry. A jewelled pendant with hinged pieces was dubbed "chimney plank," and a salacious song made the rounds of the taverns, describing in ribald stanzas the whole story of the adulterous liaison. In double-meaning verses purportedly describing the ingenious trapdoor, the song alluded to its "being apparently intact from the front / while being penetrated from behind." Madame de la Popelinière suffered through it all with unsuspected stoicism. She took refuge in a modest house on Ventadour Street and managed to survive with financial aid from the Duke of Richelieu, and later with a meager pension that the courts exacted from the spiteful husband after a long legal battle. Things did not go well for her after the disastrous *affaire*. Although the duke continued to visit her sporadically, the flame of a passion that had occasioned so much woe dimmed in the end. She died scarcely three and a half years after these ruinous developments, in 1752, of cancer of the breast. One of her biographers says that she remained all her life the fervent votary of Venus, and that she tried to console herself of the impermanence and deficiency of human affections, as she had known them, by taking one last lover. Her companion in the last and lean years of her life was an abbot. His affiliation with the Church prompted the biographer to say that she may have died unrepentant but, in all likelihood, not unconfessed.[4]

Love and lust thrive in the dark. Insofar as they share this characteristic, we are not compelled to make distinctions in the present essay. But the need for secrecy in lust is an inherent and fundamental part of its physiology. This is why the supreme sensualist is ascetic in his ways and monastic in his approach to sex: He is a Trappist, a hermit recluse in his cell, where he retires with nothing but the object of his worship.

Recall that pathologic voluptuaries bury themselves alive. The four libertines of Sade's *120 Days in Sodom* lock themselves up with their harem inside a forbidding castle deep in the Black Forest. Just where is Silling Castle, and how does one get there? It is in a remote, inaccessible site. We cannot but remember Jean Paulhan's paradoxical statement that Sade wrote fairy tales: His placement of the castle has all the trappings of a fairy tale. To reach this castle you must first go through a hamlet·controlled by smuggler-brigands who will cut your throat and rob you before they grant you the right of way. You must then climb a high, steep mountain and cross a bridge that spans a vertiginous precipice. The bridge, of course, has been destroyed by the libertines, who wished to ensure the isolation required for their perverse pleasures. If you succeed in crossing, you may discover the imposing structure in the middle of the forest. It is surrounded by a deep moat, and the drawbridges are lifted. But perhaps a good fairy assists you, as she assists the Knights of Temperance in all fairy tales. In that case, you will cross the moat and stand in front of impregnable battlements, stone walls twenty feet deep. You escalate these obstacles and find yourself in the inner yard. There is a door, through which you reach stairs that descend along tortuous, frightfully dark passages toward the secret chamber in which the hermit-libertines officiate during their abominable services of debauch. You cannot enter: The door to the inner chamber has been destroyed and in its place a brick wall has been raised. Sade's evil libertines have chosen immurement as the most effective way to segregate themselves from the world outside. The cries and howls of the victims, the exclamations of pleasure-pain and pain-pleasure of this singular group, cannot be heard from outside. And to add a final poetic touch to this unique fairy tale, Sade tells us that tons of snow are softly falling on this remote, forbidding, fortresslike château.

I have long learned that the personages of fiction are endowed with a more real kind of reality than any granted to flesh-and-blood beings. It no longer bothers me to hear it said that examples drawn from fiction are idle and that a writer's effectiveness is enhanced by quoting instances from so-called real life. The fallacy in such a statement is plain to me, but I believe·this is not the proper place to expatiate on this subject. I was already satisfied with bringing the personages of Sade to bear on the matter of secrecy among voluptuaries when another example obtruded itself from the world of everyday life. Early in 1986 the *Chicago Tribune* published an article on the sale of the State Street mansion of the noted millionaire and owner of the Playboy Corporation, Hugh Hefner. The text of the article was illustrated with photographs of the house, now transformed into an art school and residence for art students. It was inevitable that I should think of a parallelism between the State Street house and the château of Silling, although the comparison reveals the former as somewhat pedestrian and unimaginative.

The same dominant idea: Voluptuousness is to be enjoyed in undistracted concentration, like that of an anchorite absorbed in prayer. Therefore, Hefner orders the construction of hidden tunnels, secret passageways, and bookcases that move at the touch of a button. All the modern conveniences are there: He does not swim but has an indoor swimming pool, and a steambath, and a bowling alley. From his underwater bar, he can glance at the beautiful "bunnies" who swim, naked, in the glass-encased swimming pool. Panels that move by electrical mechanisms allow him to look into hidden grottoes, where his party guests give themselves freely to sexual activities. There are several hundred films in his library that he can watch at leisure in any of several projection halls. His private residence may be entered with much less effort than required to enter the château of Silling simply by crossing electrically operated iron gates guarded by security men. Once inside, one finds that the windows have been shaded, the panels draped, and the walls soundproofed. A numerous domestic service, composed of male butlers in dark suits, ensures twenty-four-hour-a-day food service in the mansion. Therefore, Hefner reveals himself as a man faithful to the voluptuaries' tradition: He renounces the outside world and lives permanently locked up within his own artificial world, oblivious to time and not knowing whether the sun is shining or whether it is night outside.

The example, as I said, appears flat in the comparison. The Marquis de Sade's creatures were awe-inspiring personages exploring the outward fringes of mind and life: the murky, dreadful zone of our being where sensuality becomes agony; pleasure, pain; and life, death. If we could have entered Silling Castle's *sancta sanctorum*, we would have beheld none other than the Malignant One, sitting on a high chair and directing the Black Mass according to the evil gospel of *120 Days*. But if we had penetrated into the State Street mansion in its heyday and reached its mirrored inner sanctum (Hefner's bedroom), we might have been disappointed. Instead of the devil revealing the terrifying forces of death and destruction that lurk in the depths of the erotic impulse, we would have seen a middle-aged American male carousing with one or more young and attractive females on a circular bed that could rotate and shake by activating the appropriate controls. And instead of being seized by panic, we would have been slightly amused at the childish heedlessness of these people who, though reared in Protestantism and the work ethic, had somehow hit upon the extraordinary notion that sex contains no elements of pathos, no germs of anguish, and not even troubling emotional content; and that, therefore, sex can be turned into an utterly trivial and pleasurable activity, to be enjoyed with the same rash unconcern with which one eats ice cream.

NOTES

Eros Ambiguous, or the Obscure Object of Desire

1. For a biologist's view on sex and evolutionary theory, see T. Ghiselin, *The Economy of Nature and the Evolution of Sex* (Berkeley: University of California Press, 1974).

2. David Crews and Michael C. Moore, "Evolution of Mechanisms Controlling Mating Behavior," *Science* 231 (Jan. 10, 1986): 121-125.

3. Scholars do not agree on the exact meaning of this passage from Dante. Some give strictly technical explanations beyond the astronomical competence of the average reader, while others attribute a purely symbolic meaning to the quoted verses. I quote from André Pézard: "During the season at which the poet undertook his trip, the sun turns exactly towards the equator. Therefore, the colure and the equator form a cross whose lines are perfectly perpendicular. Likewise, the sun's trajectory cuts the circle of the horizon at a right angle, toward the Orient (Dante is not concerned with the Occident).

Lastly, a third cross is formed in its encounter with the ecliptic." Having stated this, Pézard demonstrates that this explanation is technically inaccurate, and considers alternatives with the aid of diagrams. See Pézard's commentaries and notes to the French translation of Dante's complete works, *Dante Oeuvres Complètes Bibliothèque de la Pléiade* (Paris: Gallimard, 1985). In particular, *Appendix to Paradiso,* I, 39:1699. Other expositors are less inclined to scientific-astronomical disquisitions. To the Reverend John S. Carroll, "The four circles and the three crosses are, allegorically, the four cardinal and the three theological virtues—changed now from the form of nymphs in which he [Dante] saw them in the Earthly Paradise to their celestial equivalents." *In Patria: An Exposition of Dante's Paradiso* (London: Hodder and Stoughton, date not stated [prologue signed 1911]).

4. E. M. Kurtz, D. R. Sengelaub, A. P. Arnold, "Androgens Regulate the Dendritic Length of Mammalian Motoneurons in Adulthood," *Science* 232 (Apr. 18, 1986): 395-398.

5. All references to Jean-Paul Sartre in this essay are from his work *Being and Nothingness. L' Etre et le Néant* (Paris: Gallimard, 1970).

6. See the complete works of the Marquis de Sade, published as *Oeuvres Complètes du Marquis de Sade* (Paris: Cercle du Livre Précieux, 1967). The quotation is from *Voyage d'Italie: Florence* 15:156.

7. Quoted by Jean Molino: "Le Mythe de l'Androgyne" in *Aimer en France: 1760–1860,* vol. 2 (Clermont-Ferrand, France: Association des Publications de la Faculté de Lettres et Sciences Humaines, 1980).

8. Statement made to *Time* magazine (Aug. 18, 1986) by Betty Friedan.

9. Interview to *La Stampa* literary supplement *Tuttolibri* (Torino, Italy) July 26, 1986.

10. The controversial book of Elisabeth Badinter is *L'Un Est L'Autre* (Paris: Odile Jacob, 1986).

11. Elisabeth Badinter: *L'Amour en Plus.* (Paris: Flammarion, 1980).

On Male Jealousy

1. Jealousy as a characteristic of the Maker was accepted by the most revered Catholic exegetes. Thus, Francis Bacon stated in *Ser-*

mones Fideles, III: *De Unitate Ecclesia:* "Among the attributes of the true God it is posited that He is a jealous God; his cult suffers neither mixture, nor company." *(Inter attributa autem veri Dei ponitur quod sit Deus zelotypus; itaque cultus eius non fert mixturan, consortium.)*

2. A. W. Von Schlegel, quoted by Americo Castro in *Algunas observaciónes acerca del concepto del honor en los siglos XVI y XVII.* Revista de Filología Española. 3 (1916): 1-50, 357-386.

3. L. de Viel-Castel, *De l'honneur comme ressort dramatique.* Revue de Deux Mondes. 25 (1841): 397-421.

4. The representation of Moses as a horned individual is a curious error due to a mistranslation. In the Vulgate, a Hebrew verb meaning "to emit rays" (derived from a word meaning "horn" but also "ray of light") was improperly rendered into Latin. [See *The Principal Works of St: Jerome,* translated by Freeman (The Christian Literature Co., 1893). Footnote to Book II, 15 of *Against Jovinianus.*] To ancient Hebrews, animal horns meant only trumpets (Josh. 6:4, 13) or receptacles for carrying oils (3 Kings 1:39; 1 Sam. 16:1). However, in Holy Scripture the word is more often used in a symbolic than in a literal sense. The horn is a symbol of strength (Deut. 33:17), arrogance (Ps. 74:5-6), fierceness, or power (Jer. 48:25).

5. Achille Campanile, *La moglie ingenua e il marito malato* (Milan: Rizzoli, 1984).

The Remedies of Love

1. "The lover, betrayed by his beloved, / Wishes to heal in just one day? / Let him love elsewhere; love itself / Is the remedy of love." Marivaux (author's translation).

2. We find a reference to this Pylades, who, judging by his popularity with the fair sex, must have been the ancient Greek equivalent of Mikhail Baryshnikov, in Plutarch's *Questiones Convivales (Table Talk)* VIII:8, 712. Pylades authored a book on dancing, and together with Bathyllus developed the "tragic dance." Diogenianus, one of the convives in Plutarch's *Table Talk,* would ban this form of entertainment from banquets.

3. I am referring to Benito Jerónimo Feijóo y Montenegro, in

his essay *Remedios de el Amor*. Biblioteca de Autores Españoles, 56 (Madrid: M. Rivadeneyra, 1863): 416-428.

4. Flight by the help of birds has a very ancient history in all literatures. A semilegendary history claims that an Iranian king tried to soar by fastening eagles to his throne. Besides references to Cyrano de Bergerac, Defoe, Swift, and many others, the reader interested in this subject would do well to consult "Flight by the Help of Fowls," chapter three in *Voyages to the Moon* by Marjorie Hope Nicolson. (New York: The MacMillan Co., 1948).

5. Charles Baudelaire, "Choix de maximes consolantes sur l'amour," in *The Complete Works of Baudelaire*. (Paris: Gallimard, 1975): 548.

The Divine Marquis

1. Jean Paulhan, "La Douteuse Justine Ou Les Revanches De La Pudeur," in *The Complete Works of Sade,* published as *Oeuvres Complètes de D. A. F. de Sade*. Vol. 1 (Paris: Jean Jacques Pauvert, 1959).

2. Gilbert Lely, *Sade, Etudes Sur Sa Vie Et Sur Son Oeuvre*. (Paris: Gallimard, 1967): 92.

3. Roland Barthes, *Sade, Fourier, Loyola*. (Paris: Editions du Seuil, 1971).

4. Simone de Beauvoir, *Faut-il brûler Sade?* (Paris: Gallimard, 1955).

Some Views on Women, Past and Present

1. The superb translation by M. D. MacLeod, Lucian's dialogue is entitled "Affairs of the Heart," in *The Complete Works of Lucian*. Vol. 3 (Cambridge: Loeb Classical Library, Harvard University Press, 1967).

2. Plutarch, *Dialogue on Love (Amatorius)*. English translation by Edwin L. Minar, Jr., F. H. Sandbach, and W. C. Helmbold. (Cambridge: Loeb Classical Library, Harvard University Press, 1967.)

3. *The Prose Salernitan Questions,* edited by Brian Lawn from a Bodleian manuscript (Auct. F. 3. 10). An anonymous collection dealing with science and medicine, written by an Englishman *circa* 1200.

(Auctores Britannici Medi Aevi. V) (London: The British Academy, Oxford University Press, 1979.)

4. Régine Pernoud, *Pour En Finir Avec Le Moyen-Age* (Paris: Seuil, 1977).

5. Richard Burton, *Love, War, and Fancy: The Customs and Manners of the East from Writings on the Arabian Nights,* edited and introduced by Kenneth Walker (London: William Kimber, 1964): 126-127.

6. Morris E. Opler, "The Themal Approach in Cultural Anthropology and Its Application to North Indian Data," *Southwestern Journal of Anthropology.* 24 (1968): 215-227.

7. Pauline Kolenda, "Pox and the Terror of Childlessness: Images and Ideas of the Smallpox Goddess in a North Indian Village," chapter 11 in *Mother Worship: Theme and Variations,* edited by James J. Preston (Chapel Hill: The University of North Carolina Press, 1982) 227-250.

8. Charles Baudelaire, *Eloge du maquillage. The Complete Works of Baudelaire,* published as *Oeuvres Complètes* (with notes by Claude Pichois). Vol. 2 (Paris: Gallimard, 1975). The same text may be read in English translation in *Baudelaire: The Painter of Modern Life, and Other Essays,* translated and edited by Jonathan Mayne (New York: Phaidon Paperbacks, 1970).

9. Jean Baudrillard, *De la Séduction* (Paris: Editions Galilee, 1977).

10. Susan Brownmiller, *Femininity.* (New York: Fawcett Columbine, 1985).

The Conditions for Seduction, According to an Old Chinese Text

1. Deng Tong owed his meteoric career and his influence with emperor Wen Di to the proverbial oriental partiality for the fantastic and supernatural. The emperor had dreamed that he ascended to heaven, but his flight was impeded by negative forces. In his dream, a man wearing a yellow hat and a baldric across his back had helped him to soar. The first person whom the emperor encountered after this dream, outside his palace, and answering to this description, was Deng Tong. An uneducated man of small acquirements, he made his living rowing on a boat. He would never have left this menial

occupation, but was elevated to the highest dignities of the realm owing to his physical resemblance to the person in the emperor's dream. His good fortune was not without a price. It is recorded that the emperor suffered from skin furuncles. To show his devotion to his master, Deng Tong used to suck the purulent material with his mouth, thus relieving His Celestial Majesty of the painful swellings. This revolting act has some parallels in the West: Several legends about the Christian saints describe their kissing sores of lepers, or other disgusting acts, in order to demonstrate their love of humanity or to humiliate themselves for some saintly purpose. The Chinese emperor asked his own son to do the sucking, but the young man could not bear it and evinced his revulsion at the mere thought of such an act. This enhanced Deng Tong's standing in the emperor's favor, since by his fortitude he demonstrated greater love of the ruler than that of his own kin. The emperor, however, died, and Deng Tong was accused of embezzlement and imprisoned in spite of the pleadings of the emperor's sister in his behalf. These facts are consigned in the chronicles written by the historian Sz Ma Chian (145–91 B.C.), first published *circa* 90 B.C., although the narrative refers to historical happenings that took place much earlier, during the Han dynasty. Sz Ma Chian, *Chronicles,* 5th ed. (Taiwan: Sh-jie [World] Publishers, 1978).

I acknowledge the help of my wife, Dr. Wei Hsueh, in translating all Chinese texts referred to in this essay.

2. The two ancient Chinese chroniclers mentioned in this essay are Shi Nai-an, author of *By the Water's Edge (Shwei Hu Zhuan)* and best known for this work, who lived toward the end of the Yuan dynasty (mid-fourteenth century of our era); and Yu Xiao-yu, author of *Stories of East Chou's Many States,* in which the exhibitionist prowess of Lao Ai is told. Both of these works are considered classics in Chinese culture. Yu Xiao-yu lived in the sixteenth century. The original title of his famous work was *Chronicles of Many States During the Age of Spring and Fall.* It consisted of 280,000 written characters. A scholar who followed him, Fung Lung Mong (1574–1646), worked on the original manuscript and added to it a substantial contribution so that in the end it was 760,000 characters. The title was also changed to that by which the work is now known.

3. Donald Symons, *The Evolution of Human Sexuality* (New York: Oxford University Press, 1979).

4. E. S. Turner, *A History of Courting* (New York: E. P. Dutton & Co., Inc., 1955).

Views on the Erotic

1. Works of Saint Thomas Aquinas quoted in this essay are *Summa Theologica,* 1st complete American ed., literally translated by Fathers of the English Dominican Province Vol. 2 (New York: Benzinger Brothers, Inc., 1947) and Book 3: *Providence,* Part 1 in *On the Truth of the Catholic Faith,* translated by Vernon J. Bourke (New York: Doubleday, 1956).

2. Saint Gregory of Nyssa, *On Virginity* in *Select Writings and Letters of Gregory, Bishop of Nyssa,* translated by William Moore and Henry Austin Wilson (New York: The Christian Literature Co., 1893).

3. Works of Saint Jerome quoted in this essay are found in *The Select Library of Nicene and Post-Nicene Fathers of the Christian Church,* Second Series, translated by W. H. Freemantle, assisted by G. Lewis and W. G. Martley. Vol. 6 (New York: Charles Scribner's Sons, 1912).

4. Legends, stories, and examples of fanaticism from the patristic literature on virginity and chastity were collected by William Edward Hartpole Lecky, in his erudite two-volume work, *The History of European Morals* (London: Longmans, Green, and Co., 1902).

5. *A Rabbinic Anthology,* selected and arranged with comments and introduction by C. G. Montefiore and J. H. Loewe. (New York: Schocken Books, 1974). See page xix of introduction.

6. All quotations from Indian mystics in this essay are from the French translations of the orientalist Alain Daniélou in *Les Quatre Sens de la Vie à l'Inde Traditionelle* (Paris: Librairie Académique Perrin, 1963) and *L'Erotisme Divinisé* (Paris: Edition Buchet/Chastel, 1962).

7. Sören Kierkegaard, "In Vino Veritas," "A Recollection," and "The Banquet" in *Stages on Life's Way,* translated by Walter Lowrie (New York: Schocken Books, 1967).

8. Paul D'Enjoy, "Le baiser en Europe et en Chine," *Bulletins de la Société d'Anthropologie de Paris,* 4th ser., 8 (1897): 181-185.

9. Ernest Crawley, *The Mystic Rose: A Study of Primitive Marriage and Primitive Thought in Its Bearings on Marriage* 3d ed. (London: Spring Books, 1965).

10. James B. Pritchard, ed., *Ancient Near Eastern Texts Relating to the Old Testament,* 2nd ed. (Princeton, New Jersey: Princeton University Press, 1955).

11. From the poem "Dolores" by Algernon Charles Swinburne (1837–1909), quoted by James Perella in *The Kiss, Sacred and Profane: An Interpretative History of Kiss Symbolism and Related Religio-Erotic Themes* (Berkeley: University of California Press, 1969). See note 9, page 272.

12. Jules Janin, "L'Acre Baiser de Jean Jacques Rousseau" in *Mélanges et Variétés.* Vol. 2 (Paris: Librairie des Bibliophiles, 1876).

13. B. A. Martin, "Electroconvulsive Therapy: Politics and Practice in Ontario," *Annals of the Royal College of Physicians and Surgeons of Canada.* Vol. 20, no. 3 (May 1987): 221-224.

On Secrecy in Love

1. Unable to translate from the Arabic, I deemed it second-best to use the version of Ibn Hazm's work in the language now spoken on the land where he wrote his book. Therefore, I used as my source *El Collar de la Paloma,* 2d ed., translated into Spanish from the original Arabic by Emilio Garcia Gomez (Madrid: Sociedad de Estudios y Publicaciones, 1967). This work contains an admirable prologue by José Ortega y Gasset. There is also an English version, which was the first European translation, by A. R. Nykl, *A Book Containing the Risala Known as "The Dove's Neck" Ring, about Love and Lovers, Composed by Ali Ibn Hazm Al-Andalusi* (Paris: Geuthner, 1931).

2. Anecdotes on wooing phraseology in totalitarian countries during periods of ideological fervor are quoted from E. S. Turner, *A History of Courting* (New York: E. P. Dutton & Co., 1953).

3. Donald McCormick, *Love in Code, Or How to Keep Your Secrets* (London: Eyre Methuen Ltd., 1980). In this book may be found not

only some of the anecdotes that I have used relating to secret writing codes, but also technical explanations on ciphers and decoding technics. It may be read for simple enjoyment, or, by those interested, as an introduction to cryptographics.

4. Biographical sources for the life of Madame de la Popelinière (also written Poupelinière) are: "Mémoires de Marmontel" in *Collection des Mémoires relatifs a l'histoire de France au XVIIIe siècle*. Vol. 4 (Paris: M. Barrière, 1846): 146. Charles Colle, *Journal et Mémoires sur les hommes de lettres, les ouvrages dramatiques et les événements les plus memorables du règne de Louis XV (1748–1772)* (Paris: H. Bonhomme, 1864–1868). G. Capon, *Les petites maisons galantes de Paris au XVIIIe siècle* (Paris: H. Daragon, 1902). E. J. F. Barbier, *Journal historique et anecdotique du règne de Louis XV*. 4 vol. (Paris, 1847): 326.